ON

SHANTARAKSHITA

Marie-Louise Friquegnon
William Paterson University

WADSWORTH

THOMSON LEARNING

Australia • Canada • Mexico • Singapore • Spain
United Kingdom • United States

Printed in the United States of America
1 2 3 4 5 6 7 04 03 02 01 00

For permission to use material from this text, contact us:
Web: http://www.thomsonrights.com
Fax: 1-800-730-2215
Phone: 1-800-730-2214

For more information, contact:
Wadsworth/Thomson Learning, Inc.
10 Davis Drive
Belmont, CA 94002-3098
USA
http://www.wadsworth.com

ISBN: 0-534-58359-8

Contents

Preface

    The first time I read Shantarakshita's philosophy was in 1982 when I first discovered the *Tattvasamgraha.* I was immediately fascinated by this work which seemed to point towards a synthesis of so many of the insights of my favorite philosophers. When Ven Khenchen Palden Sherab Rinpoche and Ven. Khhenpo Tsewang Dongyal Rinpoche told me about Shantarakshita's *Madhyamakalankara (The Ornament of the Middle Way)* and the *Tattvasiddhi (The Attainment of Suchness),* I prevailed on them to help me put them into English, as well as Khenchen Palden Sherab Rinpoche's commentaries. This book began as a lengthy introduction to their work which I thought better to publish separately. I am grateful to them for allowing me to use this material, and to quote from the yet unpublished translations. I also wish to thank the late Prof. Virgil Aldrich, Prof. Hyon Hochsman, Geshe Lobsang Jamspal, Prof. John O'Connor, Prof. Richard Rumana, Prof Eric Steinhart, and Prof. Ninian Smart for reading the earlier version, Toy Tung and Beth Wilber for their editorial help and criticism, Brian Fanning, Claudia Geers, Joan Remy, and Peter Tung for their technical assistance, and William Paterson University for its support during this project. My thanks to the editor, Dr. Daniel Kolak, for including this book in his series on great philosophers. Most of all I wish to thank my husband, Raziel Abelson for his indispensible help and patience. Although this study is very limited in scope, I hope it will inspire scholars to a further exploration of the work of Shantarakshita.

This book is dedicated to my teachers,
Ven. Khenchen Palden Sherab Rinpoche
Ven. Khenpo Tsewang Dongyal Rinpoche
and Raziel Abelson

Note:
I have transliterated Sanskrit words the way they are to be
pronounced. Most Tibetan words I have transliterated the
way they are pronounced followed by the grammatical form.

Introduction

Buddhism and Philosophy

Is Buddhism a religion or a philosophy? It does not seem to require faith in its followers. The Buddha asked that his disciples not accept anything as true just because he had said it. He said that one should test the truth of what he said as a goldsmith tests gold to see if it is pure. There is no belief in a creator of the universe. People are asked to liberate themselves rather than to rely on an external source of help.

Buddhism, however, is unlike philosophy because it does not encourage its followers to indulge in idle speculation about questions that seem unanswerable.

There is no time, Buddha said, because the need to escape suffering for oneself and others is so urgent. In an early text a young man named Malunkyaputta, decides to leave the monastic life unless Buddha answers questions for him about the origin of the universe, the truth about reincarnation, whether or not the soul and body are the same, etc. Buddha replies that one would die before one could find an answer to such questions. He says that if a man is struck by an arrow, and refuses to have it taken out until he learns who shot it, what caste and color the person was, and so forth, he would die before he was treated.[1] Similarly, immersed in samsara as we are, on death row, not knowing the time or manner of our inevitable death, we must spend our time achieving the transformation of mind that will lead us to nirvana.

The way to accomplish this, Buddha said, was to recognize the validity of the four noble truths and to follow the eightfold path. The four noble truths are modeled on the ancient questions an aryuvedic physician would ask when treating a patient. What is the disease? What is its cause? Can the cause be removed and the patient cured? How can this be done? Buddha's answer was that the disease is suffering, the cause is mental, that is dissatisfaction or craving, and that this can be overcome, by following the eightfold path. This path necessitates accepting the four noble truths, committing oneself to the path, using one's speech in a positive manner, good moral conduct such as not killing, stealing, lying, misusing sex or becoming intoxicated, having a livelihood consistent with compassion, making a concerted effort to follow this path, reflecting on the nature of suffering and meditating. The nature of suffering is traced to impermanence. No matter how hard we try we cannot hold on to the things we cherish. At every moment all things, even those that seem the most stable, are withering away. And on reflection, even our cherished selves change all the time. Our supposed independence from one another is on this view an illusion. Everything interacts with everything else. This is the Buddhist solution to the problem of altruism. We need to care about others as ourselves for there are no real boundaries between self and other. Concepts about individual things are imposed on reality by the mind. Our knowledge is relative to our point of view. Liberation consists in freeing that point of view from suffering.

So far this sounds only like a philosophy of life. Where is the religious aspect? It comes I believe within meditation, that is, within experience rather than logic., experience and logic being the two pillars on which Buddhism is founded. There are two aspects of meditation in Buddhism, shamata (calming the mind) and vipasshana (insight). When the mind is calm, there may arise in it an insight which cannot be put into words. It brings great joy that eventually cannot be disturbed by anything that happens. It is associated with wisdom and compassion. It is similar to the reports of the experiences of God or the Absolute by mystics in other religious traditions. Thomas Merton, the great Catholic Benedictine monk reflected that there seemed to him to be no difference between his contemplative experience of God and what he experienced in Buddhist meditation.

To return to the place of philosophy in Buddhism, one might well ask if Buddha was so reluctant to engage in philosophical debate, why are there libraries full of Buddhist philosophy? The answer, I believe, was that it became a necessity, because Buddhists were constantly being challenged, particularly by the great Hindu and Jain philosophers of the ancient and medieval periods. According to Prof. Robert

Thurman (lecture, Columbia University) Buddhists began writing down their teachings in the vernacular, at a time when Hindus thought their sacred texts ought only to be transmitted orally by Brahmins in Sanskrit. According to Prof. Thurman, it was the Buddhist rejection of the caste system that led so many of the merchant caste to be come converts. These merchants used writing more than anyone else, because of commercial requirements. Once people began reading Buddhist texts, Hindus began to write theirs down in Sanskrit. When Buddhist ideas were under attack, Buddhist thinkers had to respond. So they too began to write in Sanskrit, which was a sort of lingua franca. Debates began to be staged at the great Indian monastery universities. These were taken very seriously. Sometimes the king was present, and the disputants were often under binding agreement to have the whole university convert to the views of a successful debater.

As time went on, Buddhist philosophers took varying views on classic philosophical questions, such as the nature of reality and knowledge. Some were atomists, identifying the material world with the ever-changing interaction of unchanging atoms. Others, idealists, identified reality with a universal ever changing mind.

The Madhyamika (middle way) philosopher, Nagarjuna, returning to the Buddha's reluctance to take a philosophical position, believed that attachment to a belief in *anything* as permanent and substantial was an impediment to enlightenment. In addition, he believed it was intellectual folly to have such an attachment. In a series of arguments reminiscent of Zeno, he laid the foundation for the Madhyamika school which divided awareness into the absolute and relative level. Madhyamika means the middle way, because the purpose of the school was to steer a middle ground between eternalism (the belief that eternal and unchanging entities existed) and nihilism (the belief that there is no veridical awareness whatever). On the relative level there is cause and effect, and one can make use of Buddhist practices to reach enlightenment. But these are just skillful means that help one to wake up from the illusion of relative awareness. When one examines relative knowledge carefully, one discovers it is full of paradoxes. Absolute reality transcends thought and can only be known through meditation.[2]

Shantarakshita and Philosophy

Shantarakshita, like Nagarjuna, belongs to the Madhyamika school of Buddhist philosophy. He too believed that adherence to any doctrine whatever was an impediment to liberation. Yet he too believed that the Buddhist path was the skillful means that led to enlightenment. He found materialism to be hopelessly paradoxical. Idealism fared better in the sense that one could not consistently deny awareness. But when one tried to make awareness into an object of thought, one again encountered paradoxes. So the nature of mind was ultimately unknowable. He is said to have united the two chariots of the Madhyamika and idealist (Chittamatra-consciousness only) schools.

In addition to being Yogachara (Cittamatra) Madhyamika, Shantarakshita's school is Svatantrika as well. Svatantrika means autonomous. This school accepts that sense perceptions provide knowledge when they are experienced without imposing any concepts on them. For Shantarakshita this is not only an interesting epistemological point, but is the doorway to the tantra. Shantaraksita believes that it is necessary for most people to start with the relative or ordinary approach to the dharma, in order to ascend to the absolute view. But on the absolute level, all this logic is superseded.

As I will explain more fully later in this study, Mahayana Buddhists believe that nirvana is samsara. That is, nirvana and samsara are not distinct realms, but are rather different kinds of awareness. When sense perceptions are experienced without reflecting that they belong to objects, or that they are pleasant or painful etc., they become a special kind of cause that is conducive to liberation.

1. Burtt,.E.A. *The Teachings of the Compassionate Buddha* New York: Mentor, 1981

2. Nagarjuna *Mulamadhyamakakarika (The Fundamental Wisdom of the Middle Way)* Translation and Commentary by Garfield, Jay L. Oxford: Oxford University Press,1995

1

Shantarakshita
Life and Lineage

The Life of Shantarakshita

Sometimes in a philosophical tradition a figure appears that stands as the culmination of what has gone before. Many would choose as such figures Aristotle, Averroes, Maimonides, St. Thomas Aquinas, Kant, and Bertrand Russell. In the Buddhist tradition, I would designate Shantarakshita for this role. An expert on non-Buddhist as well as Buddhist schools of thought, he was critical of all of them, yet not nihilistic. Like Kant, he was a critical idealist, holding the phenomenal level to be of the nature of mind, only relatively true, and affirmed the absolute level to be truly real, yet unknowable through our conceptual understanding. Unlike Kant, however, he believed that through meditation non-conceptual awareness of the absolute was possible and that this provided us with an experience that inspires our lives with wisdom, compassion and bliss.

Shantarakshita was born in Bengal, the son of the king. The date of his birth is uncertain, but we know for sure that he was teaching philosophy at the monastic university of Nalanda and in Tibet in the eighth century CE It is said that he lived a very long time. He knew of the work of Shantideva, another important figure in Tibetan Buddhist philosophy, who also taught at Nalanda University. He quotes from the *Bodhicharyavatara* in the *Tattvasiddhi*. According to Tibetan sources, Guru Padmasambhava married Shantarakshita's sister.

He was gifted in philosophy from childhood. A student at Nalanda, he became head of the university. He studied with the philosopher Jnanagarbha, and received monastic vows from him. He combined philosophic brilliance with intense religious devotion, particularly to the buddha of wisdom, Manjushri. He traveled widely, teaching in Nepal, China and East Turkistan (Liyul), and perhaps in Korea and Japan. He is most famous for his introduction of philosophical Buddhism to Tibet.

Tibetans had been familiar with Buddhist ideas since the reign of the thirty-third king of Tibet, Srongsangampo (Srong-btsan-sgam-po). As a result of his successful military campaigns in Nepal and China, (he even conquered Sian, the capital of China), he was able to demand Nepalese and Chinese princesses as brides. Both these princesses were devout Buddhists, and together they converted their husband.

Although the successors of this king were sympathetic to Buddhism, the first openly committed king was Thri srong Deutsen (Khri-gtsong-lde-btsan), the thirty-eighth king of Tibet who ascended the throne at the age of seventeen.. "After waging many wars, and extending the boundaries of Tibet, he became very interested in (Buddhism). He sent investigators to find the perfect Buddhist master. They searched throughout India, China and Nepal."[1] Finally Bagyalwai Lodro (rBargyalbai-blogros) found Shantarakshita, who was teaching at Nalanda.

Although Buddhist philosophy predominated in Nalanda, scholars debated freely with proponents of a dozen other traditions. In addition, Buddhists philosophers of different persuasions debated with each other, rivaling each other in their standards of clarity, precision and insight.

When told about Shantarakshita, the king was delighted and sent eight emissaries, two at a time, carrying gold for him. The pairs of emissaries kept two miles apart, because there were so many robbers. Six reached Shantarakshita and asked him to come to Tibet for the ground-breaking of their new temple. Although he was very advanced in age, he agreed to go, even though his friends advised him against it.

As Shantarakshita approached the city of Lhasa, the king came to meet him. The king asked him what his doctrine was. He replied, To believe what is in accordance with reason, and to reject what is not in accordance with reason." Then they traveled together to the place

Life and Lineage

where Semye university monastery would be built. Shantarakshita laid out the architectural plan in accordance with that of the Otentpari monastery in India. Unfortunately at that time there were a number of unusual natural disasters such as floods, storms, earthquake and avalanches, and the native Bonpo priests blamed the introduction of the foreign religion of Buddhism.They insisted that Shantarakshita leave the country.[2]

Buddhism was still resisted by the masses and many nobles as well. This was partly because of political reasons. Buddhism was a peace loving religion, and the Tibetans had been doing very well with their war-like ways. It was also a foreign religion, and the people feared domination by China or India. They also resented having to care for so many foreign monks. Tibetan conquests had caused so much upheaval, particularly in China and Nepal, that, ironically, monks had been forced to go to Tibet to seek refuge with its Buddhist king.[3] Finally, the people were afraid that the foreign religion would anger the local gods and demons, and that misfortunes such as smallpox (a very real danger with the foreign influx) and famine would beset the land.

Shantarakshita agreed to leave. This gentle scholar was suited for philosophical debates, not confrontations with demons and shamans. He advised the king to invite the great tantric Buddhist master, Guru Padmasambhava to subdue the Bonpo. What followed was a contest between magicians reminiscent of Moses' struggle with the Egyptian priests. The problem was solved, and Shantarakshita returned to Tibet. The monastery university was built. As well as establishing a school of philosophy, Shantarakshita started a great school for translators, in order that the entire compendium of Buddhist and non- Buddhist philosophical and religious studies of India could be translated. Eventually there were over a thousand translators working at the school.

Shantarakshita was famous for his kindness as well as his brilliance. It is said that he won the affection of the people by praising their tea, which was made by boiling water with tea, salt and yak butter.

Beginning with seven boys, all of whom became great scholars, he put scholarship and philosophical analysis in Tibet on a firm foundation. In the brief period before his death, he built a network of monastic colleges and trained a generation of philosophers, teachers and translators.

Like St. Thomas Aquinas among Christians and Shankara among Hindus, Shantarakshita is regarded as a saint by many Buddhists. Some

7

regard him as an emanation of Buddha Vajrapani. His style of writing is full of good humor and charm. As described by Dr. B. Bhattacharya:

He advances his arguments slowly and confidently, but with extraordinary caution, and with examples considered valid by both parties, anticipating objections which may be put forward by his antagonist at every step. These objections he nullifies as objections arise, and ultimately smashes each and every argument on which the theories of his opponent are based, and drives his adversary to a corner. He then explains to his opponent what his position is tantamount to, and proves that the only way to escape from this undesirable position is to hold a Buddhist theory or be a Buddhist. On such occasions Santaraksita is as jovial as a child and from his mouth flow examples of the best kind of humour associated with a refined dignity. His humour is seen very frequently when his opponent is reduced by his arguments to a theory which is also an accepted fact in Buddhism.[4]

Kamilashila, who provides us with an extensive commentary to the Tattvasiddhi, was an important philosopher in his own right. Shantarakshita's student at Nalanda, he was invited to Tibet by King Thri srong Deutsan, and arrived there after the death of Santaraksita in 762. The king was concerned about the teachings of the Chinese monk Mahayana Hoshang, who was arguing that to be perfectly still, without thought was all that was needed for enlightenment. Kamalashila repled that without the active participation of the mind, emptiness cannot be realized. Further if one tries to suppress thought, one is saddled with the thought that one needs to suppress thought. Only through discriminating thought, i.e. philosophy, and meditation can one achieve enlightenment. Kamalashila won a debate against Mahayana Hoshang in 743 and the Indian tradition of Shantarakshita became the dominant philosophy in Tibet.

Shantarakshita does not usually provide us with the names of his opponents, but only their arguments. Kamalashila fills in the names, quote from their works, and extends the arguments. His place of birth is uncertain, but was probably born about 713.Bhattacharya gives Shantarakshita, dates as 705-762, but there is a great deal of disagreement about this.[5]

Shantarakshita's Philosophical Heritage

8

Philosophy in India at the time of Shantarakshita may be divided up into the orthodox Hindu schools and the non orthodox schools such as the Charvakas, the Jains and the Buddhists.

The six orthodox schools

There were six orthodox schools. The Samkhyas believed in an all-pervading substance called prakriti or nature that formed the basis of everything. Although unitary, prakriti was said to contain three gunas, or qualities, tejas (brightness) associated with intellect, rajas (energy) and tamas (mass), and it also prompted the formation of a conscious individual self, the purusha, which was passive, and tended to be affected by tejas. This produced suffering. The way to liberation (moksha) was to disentangle the purusha from the gunas. This could be accomplished by cultivating non-attachment. In addition, one of the ways to do this was to practice certain yogic techniques. If moksha was achieved, then the purusha would remain in a state of peace forever. The Samkhya, like all the orthodox schools except the Mimamsa, believed that universes develop, degenerate and come to an end. Then a new universe comes from the ashes of the old.

The Samkhyas, although usually non-theistic, believed that prakriti itself had a teleological thrust. It provided everything the purusha needed throughout its lifetimes to eventually reach moksha.shantarakshita argued against both theistic and non-theistic Samkhya.

The Yoga School, from the root "yuj", to bind (not to be confused with yoga in general which was practiced by many systems), had the same metaphysics as the Samkhya, but was theistic. Moksha consisted in becoming close to God. They practiced various forms of yoga to purify the subtle body, a refined body existing within the regular body, so that a saving insight into the nature of being could be achieved, and union with God could be possible. As with the Samkhya system, the purusha that reached moksha would abide in eternal blissfulness.

The subtle body was believed to be in a way dissolved within the normal or gross body, but not so completely dissolved that it was inseparable. At death it could move into another gross body. The subtle body had material characteristics, but was very refined, and unobservable by ordinary means. It could be perceived through yogic perception. It was the abode of the chakras, centers of power, as well as channels of energy that were connected to them. Certain practices such

9

as physical exercise, diet, control of the breathing as well as visualizing deities and having devotion to them, could purify these channels and open the "third eye" of yogic perception.

The Nyaya (logic) school, and the Vaisheshika (to look for specific differences) school merged at a very early date. The Nyaya school, famous for its logical arguments, believed in a creator God. They believed each person had a soul and a body. But the soul was so abstract, that although it persisted though death, it existed afterwards in such a qualityless way that the school was sometimes thought to believe in annihilation after death. They were known for a proof of the existence of God similar to that of William Paley's "The Watch and the Watchmaker." They said that if one found a pot, never having found one before, since it is so perfectly formed to hold water, one must conclude there is a pot maker.Similarly, since the universe is so orderly, it must have a maker.

The Vaisheshika mainly contributed the view that all things were material, composed of atoms that were thought of as indivisible, as partless. A problem arose as to how these indivisible atoms could combine to form anything else. The Indian philosophers were familiar with the zero, the only number that is indivisible. So it seemed as though the atom had an extension of zero. But since zero plus zero equals zero, it was not clear how these atoms could ever be combined to form objects with extensions greater than zero. So the Vaisheshikas thought there must be a God who miraculously produced a quantum jump so that the atoms could combine.

The Mimamsa school is unlike all the other orthodox schools, because it holds the universe to be one and eternal. This is because the Vedas, being in the universe and themselves eternal, must have an eternal repository. The Mimamsas are mainly concerned with rituals as described in the Vedas, which they believe to be efficacious in ensuring prosperity, quite independently of the existence of God. Since their aim was to give a consistent account of the Vedas, they developed logic and became associated with the Nyaya. They believed in an eternal self which is a subject of experience and the explanation for the continuity of memory. They had little interest in yoga or meditation, believing only that if one followed the directives found in the Vedas, one would go to a heavenly realm after death.

The Mimamsa school produced the great seventh century philosopher Kumarila Bhatta, whose ideas about the existence of permanent individual selves were challenged by Shantarakshita.

The Vedanta (end of the Vedas) school, although the most influential in Hinduism, only achieved great importance after the time of Shantarakshita. The short life of Shankara, its most important figure, was probably in the late seventh or early eighth century. Shankara, like Descartes long after, believed it was impossible to doubt the existence of the self. For one needs a self to doubt the self. Further, the self is subject. To make it into an object is to falsify it. Thus the self is beyond conception. And one discovers through religious experience that it is Brahman or God. Brahman is, on the absolute level, everything that is. One cannot characterize Brahman in words. It is nirgunam, without qualities. One knows the world in the ordinary, or relative sense as dualistic, shrouded by the veil of maya, that is, in an illusory way. On the relative level, God appears in the ordinary way for Hindus, as Vishnu, Shiva etc. as Brahman sagunam, the Lord with qualities. Shankara, as well as Gaudapada, his paramaguru or highest teacher,borrowed a great deal of their conceptual systems from late Buddhist thought. All Shantarakshita seems to have known of this school is that they believed all things to be in reality that Brahman which could be spoken of as saccidananda, being, consciousness and bliss. I will return to Shankara later in this study.

Ramanuja who lived some time in the eleventh century, adopted some of Shantarakshita's arguments. He is famous for his defense of the independent existence of selves from God, while at the same time maintaining that selves and the universe were the body of God and that God was the mind or soul of the universe. Madhva in the thirteenth century asserted the independence of God from the world, a view similar to that of the Judaic-Christian tradition and Islam.

Non Orthodox Indian Schools at the Time of Shantarakshita

The Charvaka school shared the fate of materialist schools in the west in ancient times, such as that of Democritus. Although Democritus wrote as much as Aristotle we have only fragments. This is also true of the Charvaka, named after its founder. Most people do not like atheistic, materialistic, deterministic systems very much so they do not bother to preserve them. In general, the Charvaka school only accepted as real those things that were perceptible. Their views were similar to those of David Hume and the Logical Positivists. Some Charvakas believed in atoms, but others rejected them because they could not be perceived. They denied the validity of inference, because it could be used to infer the existence of imperceptible beings. For example, the Nyaya Vaisheshikas inferred the existence of God from the appearance of order in the universe. The Charvakas also rejected the belief that morality was objective. They were associated with immorality, but they may just have had a bad press. Their view of life could be characterized as 'live, drink and be merry, for tomorrow we die.'

The Jains were a religion traditionally said to be founded by Mahavira, a bit earlier than Buddhism. Buddha studied with two Jain teachers. The Jains believed in the existence of individual souls and bodies. Suffering occurred because the soul was entangled in material attachments. Liberation consisted in removing this soul (purusha) gradually from attachment to the body through a series of rigorous ascetic practices. Finally, at the end of this process, the ascetic would practice ritual starvation (with the permission of the teacher). The soul would then achieve moksha and dwell forever in a state of happiness.

The Jains were interested in both logic and philosophy. They were epistemological skeptics. They believed one could know something only from a particular point of view, and that assertions about a thing were always subject to doubt.[6]

Shantarakshita's Buddhist Heritage

Shantarakshita and the Origins of Buddhist Philosophy in Tibet

Tibet offers many gifts to the world. Her culture is rich in painting, sculpture, architecture and dance. Her people are skilled in many crafts, and are peace-loving, warm and energetic. But Tibet's greatest gift is her philosophical tradition, a tradition which is only in this century becoming known in the west A continuation of classical Indian metaphysics and logic, it encompasses all of the vehicles of Buddhism, and adds to them its own insights and explanations

Even a brief acquaintance with Tibetan thought shows that as early as the eighth century Tibetan scholars were very familiar with aspects of philosophy which would not be discovered in the west until Descartes. But of course, it is not important that the Tibetans thought of these things first. What is important is that they thought of them so well, so rigorously, and with such a sensitive understanding of the merits of many different philosophic visions of the world.

Tibet never forgot her debt to India, the home of Sakyamuni ,and the source of Madhyamika philosophy. This philosophy exemplifies the uniqueness of Buddhism. For it states that all forms, i.e. all that we know, are empty in nature. That is, reality transcends our ability to describe its words, to know it through conceptual understanding. Even the words of the Buddha are ultimately empty. Yet the understanding that is beyond conception is made accessible to us by them as a finger points to the moon. In this way, Buddhism avoids religious superstition, while also avoiding a hopelessly nihilistic and skeptical attitude. It was Indian scholars who brought these views to Tibet, along with their meditation skills and religious practices. Shantarakshita was the first among them.

The Nyingmapa is the oldest among the four Buddhist schools, the others being the Kagyupa, the Sakyapa, and the Gelugpa. The Nyingmapa was the direct recipient of the ancient Buddhist wisdom of India, at the apex of its splendor, soon to be destroyed in the eleventh century by invading Moslem forces.

According to Tibetans, they have actually invented nothing of their conceptual system.It is all implicit in the original dharma of Sakyamuni Buddha. But Buddha unveiled his teachings to suit the circumstances and abilities of practitioners, and these teachings continued to be revealed throughout his lifetime. He first preached what seemed an empiricist philosophy, epistemologically and metaphysically similar to the view of David Hume. But whereas Hume suggested at the end of the *Treatise* that if one were disturbed by his findings one should not fret but have a game of billiards, Buddhists suggested certain practical ways of implementing their theories in order to bring about the good of all sentient beings.

According to Tibetan sources, Buddha Sakyamuni was born around 600 B.C. in Kapilavastu in Northern India. He was the son of the king of the Sakyas, at that time, India's most powerful king. His father was King Suddhadana, - his mother, Queen Mayadevi. There were many special auspicious circumstances surrounding his birth. It was predicted that he would either become a great king or a great teacher.

Buddha was very wise and compassionate by nature. From the age of eight he was educated in the sixty-four kingly pursuits such as martial arts, horse racing, and archery. This education was completed at the age of twenty. Then he married Princess Yasodhara. He was sheltered by his father from any knowledge of old age, illness and death, in the hope that he would see no need to help others through his teachings, and would instead be a king.

13

Upon visiting three parks, south west and east, the boy encountered a sick pregnant woman, an old person and a corpse. His character told him such things happen to everybody. Sickened by samsara, he visited a fourth park in the north and encountered a peaceful monk. He questioned him and decided this was the path he should follow. Years before, at the age of eight his father had found him meditating under a tree. No matter where the sun was in the sky, the tree shaded him. Remembering this meditation, Siddhartha at the age of twenty-nine, left his kingdom to live as a hermit. He studied with Jain and Hindu teachers but remained unsatisfied.[7]

There were a lot of different theories among Hindus as to what constitutes liberation. The young Buddha fell in with a group of ascetics who believed that by denying the needs of the body, one could liberate the spirit. Probably some of them were influenced by Upanishadic tradition which denied the real existence of an individual self but believed, rather, in a sort of world soul which constitutes the real identity of all beings. Materialistic concerns block the realization of this identity and cause suffering, so by denying the body, the mind can merge into this world soul and achieve liberation.

The Buddha thus starved himself for six years. So great were his austerities that he nearly died. Yet he felt no closer to liberation than before. He ended his fast, sat down under a tree and resolved not to get up until he had figured out the solution to the problem of suffering.

The Buddha then, viewing humanity as suffering from a disease, envisioned the cure in the following way. 1) The disease is suffering. 2) There would be no suffering if one were not attached to the "good" things of this world such as riches, sexual pleasure, health, long life, etc. Craving, therefore, is the cause of suffering It can be cured if this attachment or craving is eliminated. 4) The way to eliminate craving is two-fold: a) wisdom - understanding the cause of suffering and b) leading one's life in a manner which is calculated to bring about an end to craving. Basically, this involves moral uprightness, compassion and meditation.

This seems rather close to the Stoic ideal. Want nothing, and you will be satisfied with whatever you have. So you won't suffer. But if this were the end of the story, then Nietzsche's objection to Buddhism would make a lot of sense. Why trade for a guaranteed absence of suffering the possibility of an ecstasy of pleasure, even if this possibility brings the probability of pain? Life with all its excitement and ups and downs seems so much more of a challenge to the adventurous mind then a sort of lukewarm security.

14

But here the story of Buddhism really gets interesting. What occurs with the cessation of craving is not a neutral state of freedom from pain but an extremely ecstatic state that has been called absolute bliss, joy, understanding, perfect beyond words. What is the explanation for this? The answer does not seem to be given by early Buddhist thinkers but appears much later. The final answer appears in Shantarakshita's *Tattvasiddhi, (The Attainment of Suchness).* [8]

Early Buddhists believed in the reality of the physical world, but not in the real nature of things as we perceive them. Tables, trees, humans, etc., are known through the sense which are internal to the body and subjective. The cause of these sensations, is composed of atoms or sense data. That is, some believed atoms were the ultimate reality, (Vaibaishika) but others believed atoms themselves were constructions out of sense data, and that sense data (or impressions, to use a Humean term) were the basic building blocks of knowledge. For although atoms could be said to exist, their nature was beyond conception Neither atoms nor sensation had any fixed nature, for they were in a constant state of flux. (Sautrantikas).

Thus there could be no soul, or permanent self either, for mind was not thought of as a special substance existing in a spiritual realm, but merely a sixth sense. Persons were in the same natural hodge-podge as everything else and were constructions of mind just as tables and trees.

Nevertheless, early Buddhists (such as the Sravakayanas) did think about liberation as the liberation of a particular person who reached nirvana, only upon reaching nirvana was individuality sniffed out. So it was considered a good thing to enter into the kind of monastic life in which one disassociates oneself from the rest of the world. It is true, they thought, that one must practice compassion towards others, but this is to break the sense of self, so that craving can be extinguished. One's ultimate concern is one's own personal salvation.

But the quest for personal salvation raises a central philosophical issue. If "person" or "self" is merely a mental construction, then the liberation of such a self must be incomplete unless all such "selves" are liberated. Yet it seems an impossible task to liberate all beings. So how can anyone be liberated at all

The answer to this question took many centuries to work out, and forms the nexus of the philosophical concern of the later School of Mahayana Buddhism. There was no one answer to this question of self-liberation; rather, there were many answers, each of which gave rise to further questions, prompting a refinement of the view.

The method by which both the early and late Buddhists strove to reach enlightenment is called the eight-fold path. This path is explained in different ways according to the various forms of Buddhism. The path includes right aspiration, right view, right livelihood, right speech, right conduct, right effort, right wisdom and right meditation. Lay people take vows to abstain from killing stealing, lying, intoxication, and sexual misconduct. Monks and nuns take vows of poverty and celibacy as well. Early Buddhists generally believed that one was not likely to reach nirvana if one did not take monastic vows. They reasoned it was too difficult to break all craving and attachments if one were entrenched in romantic relationships and the necessity of earning a living.

But as a result there were not very many people actively pursuing enlightenment. It was too difficult to renounce so much and many people found it both impractical and contrary to compassion to abandon their dependents. Later Buddhism developed a two-fold way of opening the path to all. The first aspect was connected with the doctrine of reincarnation and the requirement of universal salvation. Enlightened beings, bodhisattvas, chose not to remain in an isolated form of bliss, but took rebirth voluntarily for the sake of others. Through their extraordinary insight, wisdom, and power they were able to inspire others to renounce attachments and follow the eight-fold path. With their help, liberation became far easier to achieve. Secondly, the metaphysical system of later Mahayana, in its idealist and semi - idealist forms stressed the primacy of mind in the formation of an experience. Renunciation, then could be an act of mental detachment, while the devotee remained in the world, often actively engaged in raising a family and earning a living. An old Buddhist tale illustrates the change in attitude. Two monks were traveling together. They came to a wild river which they could cross, but with difficulty. A young woman was also trying unsuccessfully to cross. One monk, obeying the Vinaya rules of discipline, did not even look at her. The other picked her up, carried her across, set her down and continued on his way. The rest of the next day, the first monk brooded about the fact that his companion had violated the monastic rules. Finally he could stand it no longer. "How could you touch that woman?" he said to his companion. His companion replied, "Are you still carrying that woman? I set her down by the riverbank."

The second monk, represents the Mahayana path. The deal is for the devotee to be in the world but not of it. It is the activity of mind that is of primary importance, not that of the body. But according to the mainstream of Mahayana thought, body too is but a form of mind. This view is really implicit in early Buddhism, but it was not yet clearly formulated. Early Buddhism, after all, recognized that the mind creates the forms of samsara. Atoms and sense impressions act on the body through the senses. The body unifies these sensuous messages so that one will judge that the thing one sees as a cat is the same thing one touches and finds soft and hears "meow." This unified sense impression is presented to the intellect which puts it in the category of cat and animal in general. This is how the concept of cat is formed, and how all concepts are formed. Thus what the mind knows is relative to the way human beings think. This is already in the *Abhidharma Pitaka* the first systematic Buddhist philosophy.

But on further consideration, one realizes that it is also the mind's activity that forms the conception of "atom," "sense impression," the "mind" itself. So where is the objective, non- mental building block that divides objective reality from the relativistic interpretation of mind? It is nowhere to be found. Later Buddhism was in one sense idealist. But since mind itself is a relativistic concept, and since material reality as we know it is also a mental construct, objective reality cannot be conceptually known or spoken of at all. It doesn't mean it is not real. And, as we will see later, reality can. be known non-conceptually through the activity of meditation.

Because it is so thoroughly non-dualistic, later Buddhism is just as concerned with activity and compassion as with study and wisdom. The Vajrayana thinkers of India and Tibet saw the world not as a static reality to be rejected, but as flexible as the mind itself. Reality is already pure, but it is mistakenly seen as full of suffering and evil. The very activity of meditation removes the obstacles to pure perception and enables the primal purity to shine through.

Vajrayana thinkers see the three paths of Buddhism in the following way: Theravada sees the world as a poison to be rejected; the Mahayana sees it as a poison to be drunk because the antidote of meditation is there; the Vajrayana transforms the poison into nectar.

There is a fairy tale by Hans Christian Anderson called, "The Snow Queen," in which a devil drops and breaks a mirror which horribly distorts anything it reflects. A small splinter enters the heart of a child who then sees the world as evil and vicious. Vajrayiana Buddhists see sentient beings as sharing the plight of this child. The dharma is designed to remove the splinter of glass so that existence can be recognized as pure from the beginning.

The Development of Mahayana

There is a story about a Tibetan lama who described a certain cave as haunted by evil spirits. When a westerner objected to the tale, dismissing it as a myth, the lama replied, "Do not worry, you are an American. You wouldn't see any demons." Predispositions to see things in certain ways are not always the same.

It might be argued that if experience were so subjective, then all desires would be fulfilled. We need only want things for them to come into existence. The counter-argument was only to become clear much later in Buddhist thinking. It is two-fold: 1) Some things are too deeply imbedded in human history and culture to be mentally cast out, at least by most people. 2) Minds are not pure, so they will create monsters, evils, even when we consciously do not want them. Consider the nightmare. We are surprised, frightened, helpless. But we create nightmares with our own minds.

Buddhists did not deny the existence of these gods, demons, etc. which were so much a part of the thinking of their time. Today, too, they would not usually deny the existence of Christ or the Judaeo-Christian God in general. They do deny, however, the existence of a creator god. Mahayanists strove to liberate all and not pass into nirvana until all are saved. Mahayana thinkers argued that since all concepts are artificially imposed on reality by the mind, reality is beyond conception. This includes space and time. The self too, is a mere conception. So if the distinction between self and other is a mere convention no one can be really saved without the salvation of others.

The good karma created by the bodhisattva in seeking the liberation of all and the intention of the bodhisattva to be reborn for the sake of others, manifests in the phenomenal world as the reappearance of a person or type of person. So strong are the factors connected with this karma, that the "new" person will have the good intentions of the former incarnation, and even his or her "memories." The more perfect the bodhisattva, the closer and more continuous the connections with the past.

Early Mahayana literature concerned itself with the life of the Buddha *(Lalitavistara)* the dharma (Lotus of the Good Law) and the miracles of bodhisattvas like Avalokisteshvara. These sutras were said to be of miraculous origin, according to Tibetan historians such as

18

Buston and Taranatha. But beliefs in bodhisattvas, miracles etc. must be viewed in the context of the prajnaparamita literature.

The central idea of the prajnaparamita (highest wisdom) literature is the emptiness of all phenomena. This is sometimes mistakenly interpreted as the idea that all is nothing. But emptiness is not nothing; it is the full reality beyond conception.

This idea was already implied in the Abhidharma, which pinpointed mind as the creator of ordinary knowledge. It is true that the Abhidharma accepted the reality of the world. But what was this reality? There were endless debates. If atoms were real apart from experience, then how could we know them if all our perceptual knowledge is relative to human experience? If they are merely the smallest elements of objects of experience, how could they be different from our ordinary knowledge of the world, which, for example, is experienced as having color. Atoms are thought to be without color.

On the other hand if sense impressions are the basic units of experience, (more basic than atoms since atoms are a construction out of them) then they too are functions of mind, not of matter.

The prajnaparamita literature did not deny reality *per se*. It just denied the reality of anything one might claim was real, because that `anything' had to be a concept; a mental creation. One could not even say reality was mental for "mind" and "mental" are themselves concepts.

An apparent paradox immediately arises. The prajnaparamita literature is said to be the word of the Buddha. But if what the prajnaparamita literature says is true then it cannot really be true because there is no truth that can be expressed in words. Mahayana thinkers in this tradition embraced this paradox, claiming that in actual fact the Buddha never said a single word.

Nagarjuna's arguments

The ideas of the *Prajnaparamita Sutra* are expressed poetically. But Mahayana philosophers, well trained in Indian logic, expressed them in the form of tightly argued syllogisms. As we mentioned before, one of the first of these great Mahayana thinkers was Nagarjuna. Not only did Nagarjuna argue against the reality of the world as perceived by us, but also against the reality of causality, and thus of time. One of his arguments is particularly dramatic. If time is real, there must be a smallest unit, the instant. But only one instant can exist at a time. This, by definition, is the present. But according to our concept of casualty, cause must precede effect. If this is so, if the cause is present it cannot reach across its moment of time to bring about the effect which must come later. In other words, in an instant without extension there is no time for causal processes to take place Thus the way we have set up our concept of causality, on analysis, turns out to be an impossible, incoherent description.

But if we redefine reality so that the effect is not separate from the cause, but part of it, the situation is just as bad. If D effect is contained in its cause C, then C, considered as the effect of B, must be contained in B, and B in A and so on. But then all effects must be contained in a single cause. If this is the case there is no longer an explanation for why things happen one event at a time.6. The very notion of time as the measure of change, so essential to causal thinking, would become incoherent. Further, if cause and effect were the same, when one ate food one would also be eating excrement.

One might well ask whether or not Nagarjuna's argument would support notions of time as conceived of in modern theoretical physics. But modern physics is itself not very clear on the nature of time. One might guess that it would be consistent with Nagarjuna's views, though not identical with them. Physicists claim that space and time are relative to the point of view of the observer. There is no absolute, objective time or space. And thus if causal relations are classically conceived in terms of cause preceding effect, causality too can only be true relative to the observer.

The conclusions are the same but the ideas are somewhat different. Nagarjuna's arguments are logical rather than empirical. For the physicist, the viewpoint of the observer is inescapable. But for Nagarjuna, a good Buddhist, if the notion of the individual observer is itself incoherent, a result of ignorance, then the lifting of the obscurities due to ignorance should lead to a transcendence of the relative point of view. It is this final insight which saves Nagarjuna from nihilism, from insurmountable skepticism. As the bonds of ignorance fall away from the mind, relative knowledge is left behind and one comes closer and closer to the absolute.

This brings us back to the question raised earlier about nirvana in the early Buddhist tradition. If one extinguishes all desire, why isn't one left merely with a painless state? Why does one experience bliss and perfect fulfillment? The same question in a slightly different form can be raised in connection with Nagarjuna's ideas. If one dissolves the conceptions one has about ordinary life, why isn't one left with absolutely nothing?

The answer involves an aspect of Buddhism that makes it a religion rather than just a philosophy. To put it in Mahayana terms, there is something about reality which lends itself to being experienced as perfect, compassionate, wise, and blissful when the causes of ignorance are removed. It is not, however, as if the enlightened being were experiencing a different thing than ordinary beings. He or she is experiencing the same reality in a purified way. This is the meaning of "Nirvana is samsara."

Nirvana is samsara

An analogy with a similar problem in philosophy of art may be helpful here. Suppose someone has no appreciation of modern art. For example, consider a father who wants his son to go out and work to make money for the family instead of going to art school. He sees a copy of a drip painting by Jackson Pollack in his son's book. He is enraged that his son is wasting his time on studying what he sees as gobs of ink on canvas.

Then one rainy day, father and son are having a warm and friendly conversation at home. The large living room window is covered with raindrops. As the rain ends, the sun comes out and turns the raindrops into a rainbow of color. The father notices the beauty of this The son says, "That is the point of the Pollack painting." The father, understanding the value of the interplay of color and form, "sees the picture-" His perception of modern art has been purified and transformed. It is not that he is looking at a different thing when he sees the Pollack painting. He looks at the same thing but his perception is now aesthetic rather than purely physical. This analogy is helpful in many ways and we will return to it again.

Similarly, when a person achieves a high degree of realization, he or she perceives the same reality, but transformed. There is an important point at which, however, the analogy fails. In the example of the painting, there is a material object that can be viewed from a physical point of view (oil paint on canvas) or an aesthetic point of view (beautiful). But in the case of Nagarjuna's absolute level, "thing" is itself a concept which must be discarded.

Nevertheless, the analogy holds in another way. Even though the aesthetically sensitive person's appreciation of a work of art is through his or her mind and seems (and thus is in this sense) subjective it is an objective fact that certain objects lend themselves more readily than others to be perceived as beautiful. Botticelli's "La Primavera", for example, is more readily perceived as beautiful than yesterday's discarded banana peel. Those who fail to see the beauty of this painting might appropriately be called "aspect blind." Perhaps something is keeping them from enjoying the painting. Maybe, for example, they hate anything that involves pagan themes.

Mahayana Buddhists are in effect saying that the enlightened person is to the unenlightened as the aesthetically sensitive person is to one that has no enjoyment of beauty. It is not that they are experiencing a different reality but the same one in a different way. And just as it is an objective fact that "La Primavera" lends itself to being perceived as beautiful by the aesthetically sensitive, so the Buddhists in the later tradition claim it is an objective fact about reality as a whole that it lends itself to being experienced in a special way by the religiously sensitive.

Nagarjuna made explicit the distinction between the absolute and relative level contained in the prajnaparamita literature. But although his work is not at all nihilistic, it disturbed many Buddhists who worried that if the Buddha's words do not contain a literal description of reality, then they are useless. And this would seem to be the case if Nagarjuna is right that reality is not describable in any words whatsoever.

There is, however, a solution to this problem. It was worked out slowly in many stages. An important step towards the understanding of this connection was taken by Asansga and his brother Vasubandhu representing two distinct idealist trends in Buddhist thought. Both were intrigued by the ability of the mind to know the world. The mind comes to know primarily through sensation; sensations of colors, etc. which could be called external sensations, and sensations of feeling such as pain which could be called internal sensations. Given the type of mind, human, animal, etc., these sensations are organized in various ways. And humans then reason about these organized sensations and produce a conceptual system.

Idealism

Asanga and Vasubandhu two fourth century Buddhists, accepted the view that there has to be both a knower and an object of knowledge. But is the knower one or many? Are the objects one or many? And are the objects and the knower metaphysically (really) different as well as epistemologically (known to be) different?

Both concluded that the object of knowledge is not of the world itself, but is a mental construct.. It is certainly useful. It helps us get around like a blind man's stick. But what about the mind itself? Is it too a mental construct? Can one reason from the tautological fact that nothing can be experienced without being experienced, to the conclusion that everything that is, is experienced? Asanga, admitting that we only know reality through experience, concludes that this is true of the mind as well. The categories of experience that include number, object, etc. cannot be applied in a non relativistic manner to that which knows. Mind, therefore, cannot be claimed in any absolute sense to be one or many, subject or object, material vs. immaterial, etc. Asanga then, falls short of claiming that mind alone exists. But neither is mind simply a subjective entity that can be contrasted on the relative level with another non-mental reality. This is because self and other are categories which the mind imposes on things. These distinctions are not part of the world. All distinctions arise from mind, but the distinctions themselves are not part of the original flow of consciousness. Consciousness is like a river dividing into two tributaries of subject and object. Strictly speaking, it is not even correct to call this river "mind." It is simply the system of causality, of interdependent co-origination. By analogy, when one sees a mirage of water in the road, this is a trick played on the mind. Yet it occurs because of the causal interaction between the optical nerve, brain, light, road surface, etc. Similarly, experience is a result of the interplay of causal conditions which results in the "mirage" of subject and object.

Linguistic analysts such as G. E. Moore criticized idealists for views like this claiming that if, for example, time were unreal, then we would have no right to talk about someone being early for an appointment. But Buddhists such as Asanga would argue that on the level of the mirage (relative level) there are distinctions to be made such as "early" and "late." One is only in error when one tries to conceive of these concepts non relativistically Early and late, hot and cold etc. all derive their meaning from a web of interconnected concepts on the relative level. On this level they are perfectly valid. Nor is it surprising that this "walking with a stick" is so successful. Myself as subject and my seeing the cat are both spun by the same web of interdependent causes.

Let's return to the question of the validity of Buddhist scriptures. The analogy with aesthetic experience is again useful. There are certain non-aesthetic experiences which may be said to be particularly helpful in acquiring an aesthetic sense. The feel of soft sand, the sound of the sea, the warmth of the sun, while not in themselves aesthetic are likely to lead to an aesthetic experience. Similarly, the words of the Buddha are of such a nature (although themselves not absolute) as to lead to an experience of the true nature. This is their function in the system of inter-dependent co-origination, i.e., cause and effect.

Of course, no one could know for sure that the Buddhist path does lead to an experience of the true nature without actually succeeding in having this experience. Similarly, one cannot know for sure that anyone can have an experience of beauty unless one experiences beauty for oneself. All philosophy can do is to show that various perspectives on reality are possible. The proof that a given perspective may be taken must remain a matter of personal discovery. Otherwise, the result of non-conceptual meditation aimed at transcending relativistic concepts could not be distinguished from a dreamless sleep or simple self-extinction. On the contrary, the enlightenment state is filled with qualities which elude description, because our linguistic categories are meaningful only on the level of ordinary points of view.

The experience of emptiness, or the true nature, while transcending attempts to describe it, is something similar to perfect unending bliss, without suffering or difficulty of any kind. Just as physical bliss, aesthetic bliss, psychological and moral bliss, though different, are not totally dissimilar to one another, so enlightenment bliss bears some similarity to bliss on the other levels.

But if this is the true nature, and all the miseries of our world result from distorted, incomplete perceptions, how did these inadequacies arise in the first place? After all, they do not exist apart from the true nature.

The answer to this question was provided in Buddhism in terms of two concepts, that of the six poisons affecting the mind, and the related idea of the alaya or storehouse consciousness. As mentioned earlier, it is craving and ignorance which produce the idea that reality is made of material objects and that we are material beings. Anger, hatred, jealousy and fear reinforce these ideas even more strongly.

Starting at birth we have the tendency to perceive the world and ourselves in material, and spatial terms. Why is this the case? Past karma determines a lot of the way we begin to see the world. Buddhist thinkers would have understood genetic inheritance, particularly of personality, in karmic terms. But even reincarnated saints see the world materially, unless they are at the very highest levels.

All sentient beings, then, share a common unconscious mind, called the alaya or storehouse consciousness. This is a bit similar to Jung's collective unconscious. These unconscious conceptions about the nature of things are so deeply imbedded in the mind that it takes a fully enlightened being to see through them and in doing so gain some control over the karmic forces affecting himself or herself and other people.

Ordinary bodhisattvas can transform their conscious minds into a pure perception of experience by means of certain mental exercises which we will discuss later. They can even help others to do this. And with the help of perfectly enlightened beings they can even begin to affect the alaya.

There exist two forms of the alaya, pure and impure. The impure alaya consciousness is that which is inherited by sentient beings through the working of karma, in particular as the result of the five poisons. The pure alaya is the original perfect state of mind, unaffected by these poisons. With the pure alaya, subconscious nightmares are dispelled and replaced by images of beauty, peace and wisdom.

Thus Buddhist Mahayana idealism, called the Chittamatra or "mind only" school provides the answer to a central problem of idealism. Experience is mental, yet resists change, because of the alaya consciousness.

This may seem less strange if one reflects on the nature of dreams. In a nightmare, no one would deny that it is one's own mind that creates the experience. Yet one can be surprised by terrifying images. Mahayana idealism sees all of experience, when not transformed into pure awareness, as one huge nightmare. If one could image transforming and controlling one's own nightmares, one could imagine the task of the Buddhist practitioner in transforming all of his or her waking and sleeping experience. The difference is, of course, that the bodhisattva considers the nightmares of all beings as his or her own and will not rest until the experience of all sentient beings is transformed.

Asanga, agreeing with Nagarjuna that the nature of all things is emptiness, attempts to explain the way in which emptiness manifests itself. It manifests itself as mind, pure from the beginning. But because of the five poisons, experience has become corrupt and degenerate. (There is a disagreement among scholars on whether or not Asanga and Vasubandhu thought of the mind as absolutely real or rather that its nature is emptiness. It seem clear, however, that the Chittamatra thinkers against whom Shantarakshita is arguing. thought of the mind as having ultimate existence.)

But now the question remains as to why the five poisons should ever have come about from the perfect manifestation of emptiness. The answer is subtle and paradoxical and really only becomes clear later in the Vajrayana tradition in which the poisons themselves are seen in a transformed way as wisdoms.

Yet the answer is also already implicit in the Madhyamika school of Nagarjuna and the Chittamatra school of Asanga. If the nature of reality is emptiness, then since emptiness is perfect, all beings are already perfectly enlightened although they do not realize it. This idea is understood at least to some extent in the following way. Through the operation of karma, all beings are led throughout their various lifetimes to an understanding of the true nature. All eventually will reach enlightenment. But since time, space and number are applicable only on the relative level, on the absolute level enlightenment already exists. Thus to the enlightened mind all evil, illusion, etc. are seen as not existing on the absolute level.

This has exposed late Buddhist thought to the criticism that the Buddhist practitioner would see, for example, Hitler as good, and approve the genocide of the Jews. The answer to this objection necessitates an understanding of the way in which concepts operate on different perspectival levels. First it is necessary to distinguish between indigenous predicates and borrowed predicates.

A predicate is indigenous within a perspective if it acquires its original meaning from that perspective. For example, on the physical object level, heavy, balanced fat, etc. are indigenous predicates. A predicate is borrowed if its original meaning is derived from one perspective but is used in a new way on another. For example, "balance" in art is borrowed from physics. It has a new meaning, however. This is shown from the fact that if we say of a picture that it is nicely "balanced" we would not place it on the sill of an open window on the grounds that because it balanced it will not fall down. Further, someone who lacked the aesthetic perspective might not be at all clear about what we meant when we said the painting was balanced.

"Rotten" is a physical indigenous predicate. If we say an action is rotten, this is borrowed. We do not try to cut out the rottenness from the action the way we would cut it out of a peach. "Cruelty" is indigenous to the moral perspective. We punish cruel people but not cruel paintings.

Similarly, when we say "reality is good" on the level of the religious perspective, we do not mean the same thing as on the moral perspective. A good person on the moral level will struggle unrelentingly against cruelty. Not so on the absolute level. There is no point to punishment on this perspectival level any more than there would be to punishing a painting of Hitler. An unenlightened person cannot even know clearly what it means to say "reality is wisdom."

There is some connection, however, between the meaning of borrowed predicates and their indigenous use. That is why they are so apt. The connection is in experience. There is some similarity for example between our experience of balance in a painting and our experience of balance in nature. It is, however, impossible to state exactly what this is. It is somehow intuited. So there's also some similarity between our experience of a wise person and reality as wisdom.

Does this mean that reality is like a person, a kind of God? After all, Buddhists did visualize the universe as Buddha and each atom as Buddha? But, strictly speaking, one cannot say on the absolute level that the true nature either has or has not personal qualities. Such categories cannot apply.

Yet there are meditation techniques which direct one to visualize the universe as the body of Buddha, all sounds as the voice of Buddha, and all thoughts as the thoughts of Buddha. There is no doubt that this person - like imagery is very forceful. It instills devotion, which encourages effort, patience, courage, strength. Yet, ultimately, it is only skillful means, pointing to what is nameless.

There is, therefore, no contradiction between the religious assertion that reality is wise, perfect, good and the moral assertion that evil exists and we must do all we can to eliminate it. One must not confuse the perspectives. To do so would be like someone saying, "This painting is light so I can throw it in the lake and it won't sink." Rather one's very appreciation of the lightness of the painting will make one take care that it never falls into the water. One's appreciation of reality on a religious level will, therefore, inspire one to take care of all the other levels. The more complex levels of experience enrich the simpler ones, --the religious enriching the moral and aesthetic and these in turn enriching physical perceptions. On the absolute level the bodhisattva would see all things as good, yet on the relative level, spontaneously act to eliminate all of Hitler's evil ways and deeds. This explains the Buddhist injunction to have a view as vast as the sky and moral conduct as fine as a grain of sand.

Now to return to the question of the truth of the scriptures. The scriptures are said to have come from the Buddha. Probably some of them were spoken by the historical Buddha. But this is not essential. They, like the historical Buddha himself, are a pure manifestation of emptiness. It is, by analogy, as if one were having a nightmare and suddenly a saving figure or magic words were to appear in the dream and dispel the evil. The saving power could make use of the fiction of the dream itself to bring about relief from suffering. In other words, the scriptures or the word of the Buddha do not have to be true in an absolutely literal sense. They have pragmatic. truth. They are true if they lead beings to enlightenment, -- and false if they do not. To put it in Wittgenstein's terms, you use philosophy as a ladder. When you have reached your goal, you throw it away. That is why all the refuge prayers state that one will go for refuge to the Buddha, the Dharma, and the Sangha only until enlightenment is reached.

This point was made in another way by Nagarjuna's follower Chandrakirti. According to Chandrakirti, we can know nothing but words, and these words are ultimately without any meaning. Yet because philosophically we can prove their meaninglessness, by this very fact we will become less attached to the world of experience and go directly for the pure consciousness achieved through meditation. The very inadequacy of words shows the way to truth. And the scriptures, such as the prajnaparamita literature, which specifically state the limits of words, are of special value.

If on the relative level an idealist conception of reality is generally correct, it is not surprising that Mahayana Buddhists would expect pure and perfect elements of existence to become manifest through the transforming mental power of the buddhas and bodhisattvas. Some of these elements exist within nature such as the sacred lotus flower which is perfectly pure, yet grows within the mud. It is a living lesson that one can transcend the daily horror of human experience. This same alertness to the lessons of nature existed in the medieval west. One finds it in the symbolism in works of art in this period. The pelican, for example, appears in many paintings because the mother pelican will give her own body to feed her young. The pelican thus becomes a symbol of Christ. The medieval mystic thus perceived lessons in many aspects of nature, such as the purifying effect of water, the power of light to guide in the darkness. In Islamic Sufism, wine becomes a symbol of the intoxicating joy experienced in union with God. Similarly, mindfulness in Mahayana Buddhism extended to an awareness of the teaching power of all things, and thus their sacredness. It was then a short step to the Vajrayana, the ultimate goal of which was not to seek an antidote to evil, but through the power of the mind, to transform one's experience of evil into an experience of perfect purity.

The Mahayana evolved from the Theravada (Hinayana) in a logical and inevitable way. From the early view that all is impermanent and that concepts are mental fictions came the conclusions that 1) nothing has a fixed nature and hence can always be changed and 2) since the mind creates the reality of samsara, the mind-related truth of samsara can be controlled by mental disciplines and techniques. To know the emptiness of this is wisdom; to control one's reactions to things and to help others to do so is compassion.

Many clearly realized, however, this development involved difficulties, --it was easy to fall into the extremes of nihilism or eternalism. Nihilism was a danger because philosophies such as Nagarjuna's Madhyamika, tempted some people to believe that because all conceptual truth was relative truth, everything was unreal and thus liberation from samsara unnecessary. On the other hand, the use of techniques such as images of deities, mantras, etc. could tempt people to think that these divine beings, such as the goddess Tara, had eternal objective reality. (Most religions believe their deities, etc. have this sort of absolute unchanging ontological status and are thus called eternalist by Mahayana Buddhists.)

Clear warnings were given about these extremes, but they were not always heeded. Mahayana teachers, however, believed that the results were well worth the risks for in this way many could reach liberation who otherwise would not have had this opportunity

Vajrayana

Madhyamika metaphysics reinforced and explained the doctrine of impermanence. If nothing has a fixed nature, if there are in reality no substances, then that explains why things can change. Further, if all we know is constructed by the knowledge based on sensation, and evil is a result of the way in which this process operates (because of the six poisons, hatred, anger, greed, jealousy, fear, ignorance), then we can construct a pure relative truth through the senses by eliminating these poisons. It follows that nothing in our experience need be avoided, rather, the way in which we experience must be transformed. One helpful image suggested by Huston Smith, in the film "Requiem for a Faith," is that of the ocean which to a drowning person is terrifying, but brings great pleasure to an experienced swimmer. But to learn to swim correctly, an experienced teacher is essential. And the techniques for transforming experience must also be taught by a "realized" person who not only can experience the world as pure but can also understand and remember the way ordinary unrealized people perceive.

It is these techniques which are the heart of Vajrayana, the lineage of Shantarakshita. While being very similar to Mahayana, it differs with respect to one's attitude towards the world. Mahayana practices and meditation are designed as an antidote to poisons in the world in which the practitioner lives. Vajrayana techniques are designed to transform that world.

One can not, of course, describe anything in terms of the absolute level. It is beyond conception. It would have to be, because by definition the absolute level is transcendent to any particular point of view. It is said to be experienced by enlightened beings, but apart from their expressions of bliss, compassion and wisdom, this level is unknown to us. The absolute is, however, described as like a crystal which throws out many different lights. These by analogy are the manifestations of the relative level

The Vajrayana emphasizes the mental space which is visualized as the palace of the deity, often complete with towers, rooms and gardens. All smells and tastes are seen as the perfumes and nectars of the deity. For example, a person living within such a mandala might seem to an outsider to be drinking a glass of water or wine. From the point of view of the practitioner he or she is drinking the nectar of the gods from a jeweled cup. The experience of the practitioner has become perfectly beautiful and pure. Finally the deity is pictured as dissolving into light and entering the heart of the visualizer. All distinction between object and visualizer disappears and the practitioner experiences himself, or herself as the deity. Eventually the deity is itself recognized in its true nature as emptiness. The visualization is dissolved and the practitioner remains in non-conceptual meditation. Finally the practitioner returns to the ordinary world thinking that he or she has done the meditation in order to transform the world of samsara into pure buddhafield for all

Here we come to the solution to the problem mentioned earlier about the nature of Nirvana. Early Buddhism provided no answer to the question about why non attachment should produce an experience of beauty, perfection and bliss rather than simply a dull absence of pain. In the Vajrayana one comes to understand that this bliss results from the nature of reality. Although beyond conception, reality seems to the practitioner to be of such a nature as to lend itself to being experienced as perfection, - wisdom, compassion, power and bliss. These are the qualities perceived from the perspective of enlightenment. The image of the god and goddess in union therefore is clearly a most appropriate metaphor for being itself. And since we are part of reality the ability to experience that bliss is within our own nature.

1 Dongyal, Khenpo Tsewang (Rinpoche) *Flowers of Expanding Joy*, Sarnath: Pema Semye Chokhor Ling, 1999

2.Ibid.

3.David Snellgrove *Indo-Tibetan Buddhism* vol. 1 Boston: Shambhala, 1987 p.381

4.Bhattacharya, B., foreward to the *Tattvasamgraha* in Tattvasamgraha of Santaraksita, Baroda: Oriental Institute,1984 p.xiv

5. Bhattacharya op. cit. p. viii

6. For an excellent study of the various Indian schools see Ninian Smart "Indian Philosophy" in *The Encyclopedia of Philosophy* ed. Paul Edwards New York: Macmillan,

7. Ven. Dongyal op. cit.

8. Shantarakshita *Tattvasiddhi* trans. Khenchen Palden Sherab Rinpoche and Khenpo Tsewang Dongyal Rinpoche forthcoming Boca Raton: Skydancer Press

2

The Introduction of Buddhism into Tibet

Pre-Buddhist Beliefs

Tibet's role in recorded history does not predate the seventh century. It was at this time that it became a unified kingdom. The center of this kingdom was the Yarlung Valley. Lhasa, a hunting reserve, was fifty five miles southwest.

The first Yarlung kings were said to be descended from heaven and at the end of their lives returned to heaven by means of a sacred cord.The early kings were considered to be god-like beings. Although the heavenly cord was said to be severed by one of these kings, an air of sacredness continued to surround their earth bound successors. Perhaps this is why it is recorded that at the death of the king, his close associates killed themselves in sacrifice and were buried with him.

Because Bonpo beliefs had such a strong hold on the minds of the Tibetans, when the Buddhist teachers came to Tibet, they sometimes used Bonpo names, as Buddha used Hindu words in a new way when he first taught the dharma in India, so the words would be understandable to the people. Similarly, Khenchen Shantarakshita, Guru Padmasambhava and the other pandits and translators used Tibetan words that were familiar to the native population. They never used language the people could not understand. So they kept the ancient Tibetan terminology and used it to explain the dharma.

The central role of Madhyamika concepts in Tibetan Buddhism clearly distinguishes this religion from all native beliefs. Whatever the native religion was it had no sophisticated metaphysics on the level of Indian thought. For such a tradition one needs a literary and scholarly base, impossible in an illiterate population.

Nargarjuna's logic, in conjunction with an idealist view of relative truth, necessitated a middle ground between externalism and nihilism. That is, since on analysis, the world in itself must be understood as transcending our subjective concepts of it, we cannot say any of the objects of religious worship are absolutely real. Since on the relative level all our concepts are created by mind, custom and habit will dictate what will seem real to us. Thus on the relative level, there was no contradiction in the Buddhist use of native Tibetan concepts once they had been transformed into Buddhist terms. This is "skillful means" Yet unlike the native religion, nor like even the most sophisticated forms of Hinduism, the Buddhists never accepted deities as either creators or eternally real. They are part of the ebb and flow of mind.

It is, of course, easy to try to see Tibetan Buddhism as a synthesis of Indian Buddhism and native Tibetan religion. But this would be a big mistake. It would be like seeing European Christianity as an equal mixture of Barbaric Religion and Hellenistic Christianity. For example, one could argue, if one took this view, that since some barbarians practiced human sacrifice, the Christian mass was a more humane version of this. But that would be to ignore the fact that the Christian mass predated the influx of Christianity into barbarian Europe. Some barbarian converts may have seen the mass as a form of human sacrifice because they were used to thinking in these terms. And missionaries may not have stressed the difference, because they were eager to make contact with the people. Traditional holidays and ritual objects such as mistletoe and solstices were incorporated for similar reasons. But it would be a mistake for such reasons to identify Christian practices with those of Druids. Actually, the most reasonable view of the introduction of Buddhism to Tibet is that of a mighty Indian seed that fell on fertile Tibetan soil, producing a stronger, healthier plant.

Vajrayana practices were made more acceptable to the Tibetan people by casting concepts into native Tibetan terminology. The Indian dharmapalas (dharma protectors), for example, were given

Tibetan names. Dharmapalas of Tibetan origin, however, were added to the Indian.[1]

Part of the temptation to consider Tibetan Buddhism as part Bonpo is probably due to the fact that in the case of the importing of tantra into Tibet, the hand fit the glove so well. Tantric practice in India was really not well suited to the culture. The caste system and Brahmin conceptions of the appropriate and the hygienic made the tantric lack of distinction in these matters anathema. If a high caste yogi was discovered to have taken a low caste girl for his consort there was a terrible scandal.

Tibetan culture, however, was more democratic and open. The people were earthy and high-spirited and in general saw no harm in the tantra. They were used to seeing deities in many special places, so visualization came easily to them. Whatever resistance they had to Buddhism consisted mainly in a dislike of its foreignness and a fear that adherence to it would offend the local deities.

The Birth of Philosophy in Tibet

Historical background

Although by the seventh century, there were already many monks in Tibet, mostly from Central Asia, India was regarded as the purest source of Buddhist teachings. It was, after all, the native land of Buddha Sakyamuni. And it had a network of monasteries and universities which were the depositories of over a thousand years of Buddhist studies. So the eighth century King Thri Srong Deutsen sent his emissary Ba Salnang (gBa gSal-sNang) to search for the sage best able to introduce Buddhist philosophy to the Tibetan people. The people were illiterate. Their temperament was warlike. Their religion centered on divination and animal sacrifice. The emissary met Shantarakita, professor of philosophy at Nalanda University and invited him to Tibet.

Nalanda was an enormous university containing over two thousand faculty members in many different schools of medicine, humanities, arts and sciences. The Indian people had inherited a tradition of learning already over fifteen hundred years old. Their books were recorded in the sacred Sanskrit language. Although Buddhist philosophy predominated at this time, scholars debated freely with proponents of a dozen other traditions. There were, as well, many sects of Buddhism rivaling each other in their standards of clarity, precision and persuasiveness. Shantarakshita agreed to leave Nalanda University and come to Tibet. In the brief period before his death he established the Indian Buddhist tradition, built a network of monastic colleges and trained a generation of philosophers and teachers. In a few years, Tibet was a citadel of Buddhist learning.

Shantarakshita was literally a treasury of all that had gone before in Indian thought. He not only knew the formidable canon of Buddhist philosophy, but had mastered Hindu, Jain and Charvaka philosophy as well. His great work, the *Tattvasamgraha* (the compendium of truth)[2] including the commentary of his student Kamalashila, is a defense of Buddhism against the arguments of other schools. It is one of the most comprehensive and subtle philosophical treaties ever written. (Since their views are basically in accord, I will not distinguish these pholosophers in this study.

The *Madhyamakalankara (The Ornament of the Middle Way)*[3] is less comprehensive. In it Shantarakshita criticizes those views which he believes deserve the most serious philosophical consideration. His most important contribution in this work is his careful analysis of the complex forms of the idealist view and his discussion of their positive as well as negative features. In the *Tattvasiddhi (The Attainment of Suchness)*, Shantarakshita reveals himself as a tantric master, and presents a transcendental argument defending the possibility of tantric realization. According to Lopez, the early masters such as Shantarakshita and Chandrakirti did not divide themselves into the schools of Svatantrika and Prasangika that arose later in Tibet. Janggwa in the eighteenth century says (as summarized by Lopez "...although the emptiness posited by the Svatantrikas is less subtle than that of the Prasangikas, it is nonetheless accurate and universal, applying to all phenomena. This cannot be said for the emptiness asserted by the Chittamatrins , for example."[4]

The question of causality is a good example of this type of problem. It is certainly a lively issue today. How can cause be said to precede effect except *relatively* when time is relative? Do modern scientists really believe that a cause *brings about* an effect when all that appears is constant conjunction of events, justifying only statistical probability that similar events will occur together in the future?

The *Tattvasamgraha*

In the *Tattvasamgraha,* Shantarakshita argues against all the views (most of which he does not identify by name) contrary to his Yogachara Svatantrika position. What this position is, we will explain later. It is tempting in describing the *Tattvasamgraha* to merely list the various views opposed to Shantarakshita's own, and present his and his student Kamalashila's answers. But this is not helpful, for two reasons. First of all, some of the views he is refuting are not philosophically important today, as, for example, the idea that the world emerged from an eternal seed syllable. Secondly, Shantarakshita, being eager to convince his opponents, is often content to show particular inconsistencies, rather than to present rock bottom philosophical arguments against fundamental principles.

On the other hand, it would be a mistake to present Shantarakshita's views only in the framework of contemporary concerns. For some of the problems he addresses, though neglected by the contemporary philosophical community, are nonetheless important. So I will try to find a middle ground between historical interest and pure analysis.

Shantarakshita's school is known as Yogachara-Madhyamika. Yeshay Day (Ye-shes-sde) (c.800), Shantarakshita's translator into Tibetan, explains this in the following way:

> In the Madhyamika treatises composed by the master, the Superior (Nagarjuna), and his spiritual son (Aryadeva), the mode of existence or non-existence of external objects is not clarified. After that, the master Bhavaviveka refuted the system of the Vijnaptikas (Yogacharins) and posited a system of the conventional existence of external objects. Then the master Shantarakshita, relying on Yogachara texts, constructed a different system of Madhyamika which taught that external objects do not exist conventionally and that the mind lacks inherent existence ultimately. Thus, the Madhyamikas arose as two types, the former called the Sautrantika-Madhyamikas and the latter, the Yogachara-Madhyamikas. Ye-she sde *Differences Between the Views (lTa ba'i khad par) P 5847*[5]

The Introduction of Buddhism Into Tibet

Further, Shantarakshita's school is known as Sautrantika (relating to the sutra) Svatantrika (autonomous), Madhyamika. Svatantrika is a complicated subject. To explain briefly, hopefully not misleadingly, the Svatantrikas accept that mode of reasoning that uses a logical argument to establish the truth of a conclusion in the mind of an opponent. For example, In western terms, "All men are mortal. Socrates is a man. Therefore Socrates is mortal" establishes the truth of the probandum (conclusion) Socrates is mortal. Svatantrikas defend their acceptance of conclusions on the level of relative truth Another school, the Prasangika, does not agree that the truth of the conclusion is established even conventionally. Although they use syllogisms, their main method of refuting an opponent is to show a contradiction in what that person is saying. Their reason for this is because they believe all perceptions apart from those of Buddha are misleading. Svatantrikas would say that although our perceptions do not reflect absolute truth, nevertheless, in the form of a syllogism they provide a sign which can lead us out of the jungle of illusion.

Although Shantarakshita's view is correctly characterized as Svatantrika, he never sets himself up in opposition to Prasangikas or specifically to Chandrakirti.6. Shantarakshita does not deny that the nature of sense impressions is emptiness. He is only saying that on the relative level they exist apart from the cognizer.

Shantarakshita and Causality

Let us begin with the subject of causality, which is certainly a lively issue today. How can cause be said to precede effect except relatively when time is relative? Do modern scientists really believe that a cause *brings about* an effect when all that is available are general laws providing predictability based on past occurrences, which give us, at best, statistical probability?

Shantarakshita's critique of ideas about causality current during his time is derived from Nagarjuna. To reiterate, Nagarjuna had argued that if we assume 1) time exists moment after moment (a moment being an indivisible instant) 2) the cause at time A (the whole set of root cause plus background conditions, i.e., the state of the universe at time A produces the effect at time B and 3) that time A and time B are separate moments of time, (A preceding B) then it follows that the cause cannot produce the effect because, when the effect is there the cause is not, and when the cause is, the effect is not. A similar argument is also used by Descartes in attempting to prove the existence of God. God is needed to recreate the world at every moment because the cause cannot stay around long enough to bring the effect into existence.[6]

It is interesting to contrast these two thinkers. Descartes takes the problem of causality, as we have set it up, with total seriousness. Thus he needs a God to "prop up" the causal relationship when it ceases to make sense. Nagarjuna on the other hand, is content to show that on the absolute level we do not know what we are talking about when we assert causal relationships. They only make sense within the network of human habits and expectations. For Nagarjuna and Shantarakshita neither the idea that time is momentary nor that it is not make sense on the absolute level.

Accepting Nagarjuna's critique of causality,, Shantarakshita also discusses the question of whether things exist uncaused. It is interesting to note that, as Kamalashila points out (commentary to text 110) no one had explicitly held this view. The sort of arguments one might raise for it are as follows: a) we do not perceive a cause producing an effect. We only perceive one thing following another. This is true for subjective states as well as external objects. Shantarakshita's reply is strikingly similar to Hume's analysis of causality. Shantarakshita, preceding Hume by a millennium, was probably the first to propose a purely empirical conception of causality as "invariant concomitance" (succession) between classes of events, not involving any necessary connections.

Shantarakshita, however, does not believe that invariant concomitance is the only criterion of causality (text 113-114 commentary) . Some things may always be present when other things are and yet not be their causes, e.g. day and night. One can know whether something is a direct cause or not by subtracting it from the causal situation. If the result follows nevertheless, the subtracted factor is not a direct cause. Shantarakshita's view is quite close to Bertrand Russell's idea of cause as a point instant (text 115). Why one point instant is ever followed by another, however, is beyond explanation.

Shantarakshita then argues that even if one could not prove the existence of causes, this would not entail that causes do not exist. For unlike effects which are invariently concomitant with their causes, lack of evidence cannot be invariantly concomitant with the non-existence of a thing: "There is nothing incongruous in admitting the existence of things which are far removed in space and time and character and hence are not within reach of any proof (Means of Cognition)" (text 120 comm.

The Introduction of Buddhism Into Tibet

A lively concern of Shantarakshita's contemporaries was the issue of whether or not the effect could be explained as already existing in the cause. This was the position of the Samkhyas, a Hindu school which held that all phenomena except souls evolved out of prakriti (nature). The Samkhyas argued that since something cannot come from nothing, all things must come from primordial matter. Therefore all things pre-existed in their original cause.

Kamilashila argues first that it is just as mysterious to understand how a uniform primordial matter (prakriti) could produce all the varieties of things as to understand how one moment could simply follow another (text 28). And, if all causes and effects come from the same undifferentiated primordial matter, how can they be different from one other? Yet, they must be different, or one could not tell them apart. One could not even know primordial matter was a cause. But if they are really different then they cannot have the same essence.

The Samkhyas predictably reply that the effect is a modification of the cause, not a complete change. But, as Kamalashila points out in his commentary, the concept of modification will not get them out of their difficulty. If a modification took place it would either involve a modification of the original "form" or it would not. If the original form were unmodified, one could perceive cause and effect simultaneously, e.g., old age in youth. If the original form were modified, the old form would have disappeared so one could never know whether or not the new form was like the original. Also the modification could not be of the part or of the whole. It cannot be of the part because all comes from primordial matter which has no parts. Nor can it be a modification of the whole because then we would have a new thing and primordial matter would not be eternal.

The Samkhyas argue that they do not really mean that the effect actually exists in the cause but only potentially. Shantarakshita's answer has a modern ring (text 20). He rejects the idea that existing potentially is any different from plain nonexisting. This is the classic western argument against the old potentiality -actuality theory of Aristotle. The oak tree, for example, cannot be said to exist even potentially in the acorn, somewhat like a small, leafy ghost. What does Shantarakshita himself mean by potentiality? Probably just that given a root cause (a seed, for example) and the right conditions (rain, soil, etc.) we will observe, after a time, the growing of a plant. This will happen again and again. To adapt David Hume's view a bit out of context, causality is a habit of mind (see (text 72 comm. "Invariant concomitance").

Shantarakshita on the Existence and Nature of God

In Chapter II, Shantarakshita discusses the claim that God is the creator of the universe. First he gives the Nayaika argument from design text 46) that because natural objects have an orderly structure, they, like jars, must have a conscious producer. (This is, of course, the famous teleological argument for the existence God).

It is impossible to do justice here to all the subtleties of the reply. But, in brief, Shantarakshita argues that when the Nayaiksa claim that the existence of order in a jar is evidence of an intelligent cause, so the order of the world is evidence of a divine intelligence, they beg the question at issue. Everyone agrees that a perceptible design must have a cause, but this does not entail that the cause must be intelligent. For example, the Nayaikas argue that just as one perceives an arrangement of parts in a temple and infers a builder, then if one perceives an arrangement of parts in bodies, mountains etc., it is correct to infer a builder.   Shantarakshita replies that it is not obvious that bodies or mountains are arranged at all, and even if they were that would not prove that they have an intelligent cause.   One would first have to establish 'invariant concomitance"(61-62) of arrangements with intelligent causes.

Further, God is said to be one, and when we look at the various things on earth that are made we find many different makers (text 81). But then we have no reason to assume one god is the creator of all the things in the world (text 73). The world is very different from God who is perfect. So it is impossible to assume god is the creator of the jar or any other worldly object (text 72). Ramanuja, a Hindu thinker, used these same arguments in the eleventh century. One wonders if he had been reading Shantarakshita.:

> Moreover, experience teaches that agents having a knowledge of the material and other causes must be inferred only in the cases of those effects which can be produced, and the material and other causes of which can be known; such things, on the other hand, as the earth, mountains, and oceans, can neither be produced, nor can their material or other causes ever be known; we therefore have no right to infer for them intelligent producers. Hence the quality of being an effected thing can be used as an argument for proving the existence of an intelligent causal agent, only where that quality is found in things, the

The Introduction of Buddhism Into Tibet
production of which, and the knowledge of the causes of which, is possible at all. Experience further teaches that earthen pots and similar things are produced by intelligent agents possessing material bodies, using implements, not endowed with the power of a Supreme Lord, limited in knowledge and so on; the quality of being an effect, therefore supplies a reason for inferring an intelligent agent of the kind described only, and thus is opposed to the inference of attributes of a contrary nature, viz. omniscience, omnipotence, and those other attributes that belong to the highest Soul, whose existence you wish to establish.[7]

As further argument against God's existence, Shantarakshita argues in text 76, that an eternal being cannot produce anything in time because it is outside of time and the changing world. Nyayaikas argued that there must be a God who is teacher, because there is no other way to account for knowledge. You cannot have an infinite regress of teachers. Shantarakshita has two answers to this: a) (text 84) Because of reincarnation, consciousness and knowledge is not completely lost (this is Plato's solution in *The Meno*) b) Saying that teaching started with a particular person called God does not get you out of the problem of beginningless "dependence on mutual teaching." It would leave the fact of God's knowledge unaccounted for. If one cannot account for knowledge, ultimately, why bring God up at all?

Next Shantarakshita introduces the possibility (held by some theistic Samkhyas, followers of the Yoga system) that the world is caused by God and primordial matter working together, just as a potter uses clay to make a jar (text 94). But Shantarakshita points out that the same objections raised earlier would also apply. Since both God and primordial matter are said to be absolutely simple, they cannot interact to produce the variety existing in the world.

The Samkhya theists might reply (text 97-100) that God creates by coming into contact with the three aspects of nature, i.e., with brightness, force and matter. Since these three aspects are necessarily consecutive in their function, their creation is produced consecutively, even though God is changeless.

Shantarakshita answers this in the following way. The capacity to perform all creative acts must be with God-Primordial Matter in an absolutely timeless way since both are simple and unchanging. But if this is the case there is nothing to prevent all their creative activity from occurring simultaneously. Indeed it must, (text 101-102) because since

41

they are changeless, no particular potency can disappear to reappear later (text 104-105).

Finally Shantarakshita attacks the position of those who declare that the Spirit (Purusha, meant as Ishvara-the Lord) created all things. His arguments are similar to those raised against the Nyayika. Most of the same arguments which apply to God apply to the world spirit. The main difference between the term Purusha and the term God is that they have slightly different connotations. God is said to be the efficient cause of the world whereas the Purusha is both the efficient and constituent cause, i.e., the world is said to have the nature of Purusha. The new arguments of this chapter have mainly to do with the issue of compassion. If the Purusha created the world, being all good, it would never allow suffering. It would create only happy, good beings and never allow them to perish. But suffering and death exist, so there can be no Purusha, as Hume was to argue a millennium later.

There is one curious argument in text 161. Shantarakshita considers the possibility that the Purusha created the world not out of mercy and compassion, but rather, was motivated by the desire for amusement. But this, Shantarakshita argues, would make the Purusha dependent on "the implements of amusement" that is creation, sustenance and dissolution of the world" etc. (commentary) The second argument is the variation of those in Chapters II and III. If the Purusha is all-powerful, he would bring about simultaneously all the things which would amuse him.

Shantarakshita and the nature of the self

In Chapter VII, Shantarakshita begins his analysis of the nature of the self. It is a different concept from that of the Purusha, which is consciousness *per se*. The self is the one that has consciousness. (texts 171-176) His criticism in this chapter is surprisingly mainly directed against arguments claiming that since all that is known is the result of a process of knowing, there must be a distinction between a substantial knower and what is known. Shantarakshita again reminds us that such a distinction involves an infinite regress (text 190 commentary). For if the knower is a substantial self who also has self knowledge, then there must be knower that knows the knower, etc. ad infinitum, which is absurd.

Shantarakshita accepts the argument that the existence of a cognizer is indubitable because it would be self-contradictory to doubt that there was a doubter. But in relation to the Cartesian question and

The Introduction of Buddhism Into Tibet

answer "How often am I? As often as I think", unlike Descartes, and Bertrand Russell, he sees no reason to believe that the cognizer is the same in every cognition. It changes as the cognition changes. It is inseparably bound up with the cognition in the momentary conjunction of interdependent conditions. Although called by a single name (self or soul), consciousness is not a single enduring entity. If it were, there would have to be a self that knows the knower each time we think about the knower. Again this leads to an infinite regress of substantial souls, which is absurd.

The Nyayaikas had argued that the self is necessary to serve as the substratum of desires etc., and enduring selves are a causally necessary condition of desire. Shantarakshita asks (text 191-192) what they mean by the cause of desire. He readily admits that desires are caused. But, he says, when the Nyayaikas assert that the self is a sustaining causal condition of desires etc. in the form of a receptacle, they are being misled by an inappropriate picture. Receptacles are only needed with things that will move if not restrained. The jujube fruit, for example, is placed in a container, so the pieces won't roll all over. But with desires, perceptions etc. there is no place for them to move to, so they do not need to inhere in anything.

Another important Nayaika argument for the existence of a single self, or cognizer, is that we are able to recall the past through memory and identify such past experiences as our own. Shantarakshita claims that the conclusion, that i.e., there is a single cognizer, begs the question. We do not know that we are correctly identifying the agent of the past with the knower (remenberer) of the present. It is possible that these experiences of perceiving etc. have the peculiar ability to produce the illusion that there is a *continuing* cognizer.

Shantarakshita then (text 197) uses the same form of argument he used in the case of God and primordial matter to argue that an unchanging, eternal self cannot be the cause of phenomena that occur in sequence. Because if the self as cause is unchanging and eternal, the efficient cause of perceptions desires etc. being always present, would produce all of them all at once. This of course is not the case, so an unchanging self as cause does not exist.

Nyaikas argued that a single cognizer must produce the six cognitions of the senses, e.g., the sight of a dancing girl, the sound of the drum, etc. because they are produced in succession.. But actually, Shantarakshita replies, the eye sees the color, the ear the sound etc. all at the same time. These different impressions of the dancing girl do happen all at once, so again, they cannot have a single, enduring

43

unchanging self as cause. (text 200- 201 comm) The Nyayaikas also formulated the very simple argument that since we have a single term for the "soul" there must be a single entity to which it corresponds. Shantarakshita replies (texts 202-206) 1) "existence of synonyms shows there is no unique relationship between word and object e.g. kava and sharira both mean "body". 2) Words are often used to refer to non-existent entities, e.g. the sky lotus. The reason this is possible is due to the conventional nature of language. We can use words to mean whatever we like: "Convention proceeds from the independent desire of men (to give a certain name to a certain thing); and terms also are expressive of that alone; wherefore then could there be any restriction of their use?" (text 206 commentary).

The Nayaikas also argued that the soul is the cause of breathing etc. and that at death, it is the departure of the soul which causes the cessation of breathing etc. Shantarakshita replies (text 206-208) that there is no well-established connection (invariant concomitance) between soul and breathing. Nor can there be, because, soul is an incoherent concept. Just as there can be no invariant concomitance between absence of the son of the barren woman and absence of breathing, so there can be none between absence of the soul and absence of breathing. Further, breathing is sequential, and soul is said to be an unchanging eternal substance. So soul could not in any case be the cause of such a sequential process. And thus, the absence of breathing at death is not caused by the absence of soul.

One of Shantarakshita's most interesting arguments concerns the Nyayaika claim that the self knows itself. He casts this claim in a Cartesian-like form: (text 212) "Others have assumed that the 'Soul is proved by Perception; because' I-consciousness' is self-cognizable, and the soul forms the object of that consciousness." Shantarakshita replies (text 212-214) that the soul cannot be the object of the "I" consciousness, because the claim is that the soul is eternal, - omnipresent, intelligent, but "not the slightest manifestation of these characters is perceived in "I" consciousness; the manifestation which *is* perceived in "I" consciousness is all in connection with fair-complexion' and other conditions of the *Body* - as is apparent in such expressions as 'I am fair, - with weak powers of vision, -lean, - beset with acute pain' and so forth." (texts 213-214 commentary) The soul is clearly not the sort of thing which can be said to be fair complexioned etc. So this "I" consciousness cannot be consciousness of the soul. Shantarakshita's opponents claimed that the notion of the soul is clear. But as Shantarakshita points out there is nothing to be

44

found in "I" consciousness that clearly has the form of soul (text 213-214) The commentary to text 220 concludes in a very interesting way. Kamalashila admits there is an "I"-consciousness and a mind associated with it. This mind is not part of the body. But like the body, it is momentary. In this sense one could call this momentary mind the soul. But "soul" does not denote a substance of any kind, much less an eternal substance.

In a modern sense one might call the "I" the ability to use the first person pronoun. In a Buddhist context, it would not be just the ability, but also the tendency to do so. It is this tendency which is the grasping aspect of existence which is the root of suffering. "Person", by contrast, functions like "chariot" as a convenient term for a collection of aggregates. Failure to understand this distinction is perhaps the reason that later Buddhist writers accused Shantarakshita of believing the *person* was real in the sense of substantially existent.

Shantarakshita then takes up the claim (chap. VII) that the self is sentience which for the Mimamsas is the same as cosmic intelligence. This view was held notably by the Mimamsa theologian Kumarila Bhatta, who believed that the self has two kinds of states, "inclusive" and "exclusive". Only inclusive states are permanent. They include intelligence, substance and being (text 222). The exclusive states are those which are experienced in mutually exclusive ways, such as pleasure and pain. The self is like a snake which coils and uncoils. It changes shape but remains always a snake. Its whole character neither disappears completely, nor is there a continuation of its whole character (text 223 commentary) "its states of pleasure, etc., go on disappearing and appearing again, but intelligence permeates all these states; hence there is no incompatibility between the 'exclusive' and 'inclusive' states."

Kumarila's argument for this is as follows. (text 226) If the soul were to utterly disappear at every moment and a completely new soul were to reappear at every moment, then there would be no way to explain how we identify those actions in the past which we have done, the *doer* would not be there to come into contact with the effect of the act. But if the self were completely unchanging, then there would be no way it could experience contrary feelings of pain and pleasure.

In text 229-237, Shantarakshita formulates the core of the Mimansa argument that the Buddhist view of the self cannot account for the temporal aspect of experience. If the object is not different from the knower, than we can never say 'I saw x then, and I see it again now. If the I is in the past we can say the former but not the latter. If in the present, vice versa. The sentence "I saw it in the past" would not be true. We cannot thus speak truly about past and future experiences as a continuum if there is no enduring self. Nor can the self be a series of moments, because a series is not an entity and only an entity can be a knower.

Shantarakshita interrupts his presentation of the Mimamsa argument (Kumarila) at this point to provide us with some useful criticism. The Mimamsa have insisted that intelligence (cognition)is eternal and one. But they also insist that a) cognitions are momentary, and b) cognitions are produced by perception. a) contradicts the principle that cognition is eternal and that cognition has no other nature but intelligence, and b) contradicts the principle that what is eternal cannot be produced.

Shantarakshita then continues with his précis of the Mimamsa argument. The Mimamsas claim that mind is eternal (text 242), because it is of the nature of intelligence. The difference in cognitions is due to the diversity of the object. Shantarakshita has objected that if soul is one and eternal it would know all things simultaneously, rather than consecutively. Kumarila tries to forestall this type of objection (text 243) by likening the self to fire which consumes many different things while always remaining fire: "Fire is eternally of the nature of a Burner and yet it does not burn all things at all times. It burns only what is brought to it; - and then also, it burns only a thing that is capable of being burnt - and not the sky or any other such thing." In the same way a rock crystal mirror stays the same yet reflects whatever is brought in front of it. (text 244-245) Cognition similarly reflects only what is presented to it in a fleeting way by the sense organs, just as the fire only burns what it touches and the mirror only reflects what is brought before it. Thus the evanescence of cognition is due not to its own nature but because it must reflect truly the nature of what is sensed. And the sense organs perceive in a constantly changing manner. This is the Mimamsa answer to the point that if the self is eternal it will perceive all things simultaneously. It would indeed do so if it were always in contact with everything, but this is not the case.

In reply Shantarakshita answers that if cognition is one and eternal, the cognition of sound in a certain case cannot be different from the cognition of taste etc. But surely this is not true. The cognition of a lemon's taste is very different from the cognition of the sound it makes when it drops. Nor can the analogy with fire be of much help. Because fire too, comes and goes. If it did not, all combustible things would burn all at once. Fire is indeed, only a burner when it touches a combustible thing (text 256). Thus it is very unlike the eternal, unchanging cognizer. Nor does the analogy with the mirror help the Mimamsa position (texts 259-260). Again we are clinging to a false picture. The mirror does not contain the image the way the self as cognizer is said to contain the thought. Nor does the mirror become transformed into the reflection. A glance at the side of the mirror will show it remains the same. (text 260) If it were really transformed into the reflection it would be different at every moment, which is just what the Mimamsa do not want to say about the soul. But if the analogy holds and one says the reflection is illusion, then cognition must be an illusion as well. But how can cognitions be illusions when cognition is said to be eternal, unlike illusions which are always transitory? (text 262)

The arguments contained in the next few texts are rather complex, but I will try to formulate them in a schematic way (texts 264-271) Kumarila has argued that the soul remains the same soul when it experiences first pain, then pleasure etc., because it contains continuously such qualities as intelligence, being etc. Shantarakshita replies that this cannot be the case. For the Mimamsa insist that the cognizer and what is cognized are non-different: "When one thing is non-different from another, its destruction and origination must follow on the destruction and origination of the latter; just like ...those same States of Happiness and the rest, and the soul has been said to be non-different in nature from the States of Happiness and the rest." (text 268 comm.) (For example, it is only if a chair is different from its state of being blue that it can be the same chair if it is painted red. If the chair is non-different from its state of being blue it must be a *different* chair if it is painted red. So with the soul. If the soul is one with its state of happiness, it cannot be the same soul if it is in pain. Further if the soul is one with its states, and the states originate, the soul must originate. But this is contrary to the Mimamsa view that the soul is eternal.)

In text 272 Shantarakshita goes back to the central Mimamsa claim that the soul's character of "doer" or "experiencer" is different from any particular state that it is in. Thus they are claiming that the soul is identical with its character of doer, and is identical with the state it is in, but its character of doing and its particular state are non-identical. Shantarakshita argues that one cannot simply have a "doer". Every doer must be a doer of something. And the doer of x is different from the doer of y. Jane playing basketball is different from Jane playing baseball. Kumarila would answer that Jane, as soul or doer, is modified when she stops playing basketball and starts playing baseball; modified but not destroyed. Shantarakshita's reply is subtle. He argues that one cannot disprove that the soul as sentience is eternal. (It is however difficult to prove it is eternal (text 305). The form of sentience, however, is always changing. In this sense the form is destroyed at every moment, and a new form reappears at the next. Jane is inseparable from Jane playing basketball. Jane playing basketball has a definite form, which is destroyed and replaced by the form of Jane playing baseball. All that remains is a formless sentience. If this is all you mean by soul (says Shantarakshita), I have no quarrel with you. The snake can only coil and uncoil because it has no permanent form. The same is true of sentience. If it had a permanent form it could never experience different states.

If there is no soul, that is a soul with a form, where do we get the notion of "I". Shantarakshita discusses this issue, one of the most important in all of Buddhism, in texts 277-280. It is simply a matter of cause and effect. The "I" notion arises only in some things and not in others,- -only in those things which have the potential to give rise to it. A jar does not have this potential, a human being does.

The "I" notion is caused to arise but has no real basis. If it did have a basis, that basis would have to be eternal or non eternal. If it were eternal, all "I" notions would exist together. That is, since the causes of "I" notions were always there, they would all have to be brought about at once. But if the cause is not eternal, yet there was a substantial basis for the "I" notion, we would be able to apprehend it as clearly as those things for which (relatively speaking) there is a real basis. There is color, so we see it. If there were an "I" we would apprehend it. But like Hume, Shantarakshita is saying that we never perceive the self.

To return briefly to the central Mimamsa position that one needs a self or soul to recognize which past and present acts are "one's own" and which are not, Shantarakshita is showing that this sort of argument is question-begging. One cannot prove the "I" exists by saying that it is necessary in order to recognize the present "I" as the same as the past. But of course, if one does not explain the belief that the "I" endures by the fact that there is an enduring "I," one must find some other way. This Shantarakshita locates in the nature of causality itself. If a momentary state is of such a nature as to give rise to the illusion of a self plus the illusion that it is the same self as existed before, then one will experience a sense of an enduring self. Why does this happen? Because where sentience exists clinging arises. And the sense of self is a form of clinging. And this produces a karmic chain. But Shantarakshita will discuss this explicitly in the following chapter.

48

Shantarakshita's next concern is with the Samkhya notion of the soul. The Samkhyas believed that cognition or cosmic intellect was a characteristic of primordial matter alone. Primordial matter is the doer of all actions, the seed of all evolution. The individual is not a doer at all, but pure passive sentience (texts 285-286). This sentience (or soul) is the enjoyer of the fruit of good or bad deeds. This sentience is one, (one form) changeless and eternal.

Shankaraksita's arguments against this position are similar to those used against the Nyaya and Mimamsa views, as well as against the doctrine of the purusha. If sentience is of one form, how can it perceive diversity? How can it enjoy many different things? How can it desire different things? For either the perception, the enjoyment, the desire, are different from sentience or the same. If the same, then this contradicts the fact that sometimes the soul perceives and enjoys and desires and sometimes it does not. So it would be modified, which contradicts the Samkhya view.

Further, if as the Samkhyas believe, primordial matter contains all that is, and "bestows the fruits in accordance with the desires of the soul," then why do not we always get whatever we want? There is certainly enough in primordial matter to fulfill all desires. (text 293) And if primordial matter brings about things in accordance with the desires of the soul, how can it be insentient?"' (text 299)

There is no reason, furthermore, to believe that sentience itself is imperishable. Our experience of it is as of something transitory. There is no proof that it cannot be transitory. If it were eternal, one would not need the senses which call it into action. If fire were eternal, we would not need fuel. By analogy if sentience were eternal, we would not need sensation. (text 305)

In Chapter six, Shantarakshita offers some friendly criticism of the advaita (nondualism) view of the self which he says is substantially correct, with the exception that they hold mind to be eternal. This Hindu view resembles that of Shantarakshita in the following ways: 1) They assert the world as we know it (relative level) to be of the nature of thought. 2) They deny the reality of the individual self. Shantarakshita does not give the advaita arguments for these two beliefs, but concentrates on disproving the idea that mind is one and eternal. His first argument follows his general attack on the idea that what is one and eternal can exist in different states. "In an Eternal Entity there can be no different 'states' because the 'states' are not different from the Entity to which they belong"(text *330-331* comm). Otherwise the eternal entity would be liable to production or destruction which is impossible. And the states cannot be different because this would contradict their view that this eternal entity is all that exists (text *330-332*). We cannot know this through inference because a) it is not analytically true that the eternal entity must exist , , nor b) are any effects of such an eternal nature discoverable. *(332)*

This looks as if Shantarakshita is committing a simple mistake. Why can't a single entity exist in different states without failing to remain one? But the Hindu view he is criticizing of oneness implies indivisibility in space and changelessness in time. And thus the identity of such a one with itself cannot admit of different states, on their criterion of sameness.

Further, if eternal cognition were all that existed, how could there be the varying states of bondage and liberation? If eternal cognition were eternally right we would already be liberated. If it were eternally wrong, there would be no hope for such liberation. This would make the practice of yoga fruitless. But if cognition is in flux, one's consciousness can change and liberation can be attained (text 333-335).

The next position criticized by Shantarakshita is that of the Pudgalists, a heretical Buddhist sect which held that there is a self but its nature is beyond conception. The orthodox view insists that the self is reducible to the skandhas (bundles, such as body, thoughts etc.). Pudgalism arose because some Jain philosophers, fascinated by the teachings of the Buddha, sought to combine them with their own notion of purusha. In order to avoid obstacles arising in their practice, Gautama Buddha chose not to take a clear position on the non-existence of the self. Because of this, some Buddhists believed there was a self, but it was beyond conception. Of course, some things in Buddhism such as the dharmakaya are beyond conception. But only those things, which are beyond conception, are said to be possible which are not provably impossible. The son of the barren woman, for example, is not only beyond conception, but impossible, because provably false in virtue of its self-contradictory nature. The same is true of the self, which Shantarakshita will show is impossible even in the quasi-real way envisioned by the Pudgalists (Buddhists who accept a quasi self).

The Pudgalists accepted the type of criticism used by Shantarakshita, namely that the self can neither be the same nor different from the momentary thought phases. For this reason, they argued the self must be beyond conception. Yet it must exist, or the Buddha would not have spoken of the "bearer of the burden." Shantarakshita replies that if something cannot be spoken of as being

50

the same or different from something else it must be formless. Because form is exactly that which differentiates. But if. the self is formless it cannot be a substance. (text 340-342) And the Pudgalists utilize conceptions of sameness and difference in talking about the pudgala. So it is clear that they mean that it is a substance. (text 343 comm.) Further the reason that the thought phases cannot be the same as the pudgala is that they are said by the Pudgalists to have mutually exclusive properties. The thought phases can be spoken of but the pudgala is incapable of being spoken of. (text 344)

This argument is followed by another which introduces some very interesting metaphysical ideas. Shantarakshita argues that the pudgala, being a substance, must either be eternal or momentary (changing). If eternal, it cannot act, because action implies change and the eternal cannot change. So it must be momentary. (A similar criticism is leveled against Christian theologians by their opponents who claim an eternal unchanging God could not bring the world into existence.)

Shantarakshita then considers an objection of the Pudgalists that the notion of the pudgala escapes this criticism, because being beyond conception it cannot be said to be either eternal or non-eternal ' "so effective action cannot be incompatible with it." (text 347 comm.)

Kamalashila here advances an argument which is part of his nominalist bent. He doesn't object to the pudgalists "calling" the pudgala an entity beyond conception, because anything can be called anything. Nevertheless, we can show that their use of this term is incoherent. Because all that is meant by eternal is that something has a nature which does not change. All that is mean by temporal is that the nature of a thing changes. So if the Pudgalists accept this notion of the eternal and momentary (to which they do not seem to have objected) then it is clear that they should accept the view that any entity must either have a changing *or* unchanging nature. But if they accept this, then they cannot also claim that the pudgala, an entity, cannot be said to be either eternal or momentary. (text 347 comm.)

One might consider at this point whether or not Shantarakshita had any knowledge of advaita (all is Brahman, distinctions are illusory) philosophers such as Gaudapada who distinguished between the absolute and relative level. For many advaitists (Shankara most notably) true reality was the Brahman nirgunam, the Brahman beyond conception. Shantarakshita does not seem to be aware of this position. His criticism of the advaitists seems to ignore their use of the absolute/relative distinction. But if he had known, he might have said (as Kamalashila said of the Pudgalists) that if reality is really beyond conception, then it is meaningless to call it the absolute Brahman or non-Brahman, permanent or impermanent. Of course you can call it Brahman if you like, but then the term Brahman is contentless. For Shantarakshita, the self or "I" is an effect of the momentary causal activity of all the skandhas productive of the sense of self. Actually Shantarakshita's position is quite like that of Shankara's. I shall return to this later.

Shantarakshita has argued that even on the relative level the self does not exist. It is an illusion produced by the skandhas. But what about the skandhas themselves? What is their nature, not only with respect to the human person, but all things?

First of all, as Shantarakshita argues in the next chapter, all things are momentary in nature. Nothing whatever can endure through past, present and future time. At first this seems like an outrageous affront to common sense. Surely the flower that one sees when coming into a room is the same one glances at an hour later. But, Shantarakshita argues, this is an illusion. All things which exist must be capable of causing a change in something else or being changed. What exists in one moment of time is what must produce the next moment of time. For example, the seed, the water, earth, sun, air etc. in one moment of time must produce the first stage of the plant in the next moment of time. If the first moment does not disappear, the next moment cannot come into existence. Thus anything which is non-momentary is fruitless, causally speaking. And to be fruitless is to be non-existent. (For according to Shantarakshita, to exist is to function.)

It might be argued that ideas, such as beauty, truth, etc. are permanent. Shantarakshita argues that this cannot be, because these words are mere names assigned by whim or habit to groups of things existing in our experience. If we want to call the sun a light and a butter lamp a light we can do so. This does not make them the same thing. If we want to call two similarly appearing momentary successive entities the same thing we can do so. It makes no difference if these entities are thoughts or external things. Calling them the same will not make them the same.

Earlier in the chapter Shantarakshita had argued that things cannot be permanent because of their inter-dependent nature. Everything is what it is because of certain causal conditions (e.g. the seed, soil etc.) which themselves depend on other things. Shantarakshita is saying that the entire system of existing things is interconnected, so that any change anywhere in the system will sooner or later bring about a change everywhere else. So nothing is self-existing. But, one might argue that the total system itself is self-existing. Although Shantarakshita does not confront this argument directly, one can see that his subsequent argument about the momentariness of things precludes this possibility. For a totality which must depend at every moment for its existence on the causal conditions of the moment before cannot be said to be selfexisting. In short if every moment of time is different from the next and all things are interdependent, then nothing can be permanent.

It may be useful now to recall the former objection that if cause and effect are momentary, the cause cannot stay around long enough to touch or bring about the effect, and that if this is so there is no way to explain the invariant concomitance between causes and their effects, e.g. the seed, plus auxiliary conditions, producing the plant and not a chair. The answer to this objection was that what we mean by cause is invariant concomitance. It is simply a name for the orderly way in which we experience reality. As for momentariness itself there is no explanation or cause. It is simply the way reality is.

Causality

The clearest expression of why reality on the relative level must be mental is found in the *Madhaymakalankara.* The analysis of momentariness is used in chapters 10-14 to demonstrate the emptiness of concepts such as substance, quality, action, generality, particularity, and inherence. These arguments are all very interesting and deserve careful attention. For want of time, we will just point out that they are variants of the arguments concerning the impermanence of things. Everything is constantly in flux and interdependent. So there can be no substance, - nothing that is independent and enduring. Qualities such as color etc. are subjective and cannot be said to inhere in objects. If they did, atoms would have color, but they do not. Nor can things have number. When you see an elephant you see only an elephant and not the elephant plus the number one. Hence numbers exist only in the mind. The same is true of generality. General terms are only a form of mental inexactitude, albeit a necessary one. No two cows are exactly the same. But we can't name every cow so we make up a name for all animals which can be usefully called by the name 'cow',' those which give milk, moo, etc. Particularity is also a myth because the only real candidates for particularity, the atoms, have been shown to be unintelligible. Nor is inherence possible. In a Humean vein,

Shantarakshita argues that since there is no substance, there can be no inherence of qualities.

Criticism of materialism

It is clear that Shantarakshita is convinced that the secondary qualities, to use a western term, exist only relative to a sentient being, and the primary qualities (measurable qualities) are relative too. What then of matter itself? Does it exist? Is it atomic in nature or made up of the four elements?

This is a tricky issue for it is tempting to "modernize" Shantarakshita. But we are not dealing here with a modern chemical or atomic theory which is, at least to a large extent, empirical. Briefly, the theory that the world is composed of the interaction of the elements runs into the following difficulty. These elements are either eternal (unchanging) or momentary (changing). If they are eternal they cannot be modified and combine with each other to form objects. If they are changing, then their identity as elements has been lost. The theory of atoms seemed the ideal means of escaping this difficulty. Everything material can be divided. But one cannot divide forever. The smallest possible bit of matter was said to be the atom. Everything was made from them. Sensations are caused by them.

Putting aside modern considerations regarding atomic theory, the ancient notion of the atom runs into the following difficulties. If an atom occupies space it must have a top, bottom, etc.. Thus when atoms interact it must be one of these directions (sides) of the atom which interacts. But then the atom must be divisible (which contradicts the concept of an atom) or it must change into the other atom (which contradicts its unchanging nature). (text 1990-1997) He does not consider the possibility of action at a distance.

There are other problems about atomism as envisaged by the ancients. The atom is imperceptible, but the tables and chairs that are composed of them are not. Atoms do not for example share the qualities of colors which objects possess. All we know is traceable to sensation. But if our sensations tell us about what is only relatively true (e.g. the color of a table) then if atoms alone are ultimately real, what our sensations tell us is unreal. So the atomist is asking us to believe in the existence of entities which we cannot see, which cannot interact with one another and thus produce change, and the existence of which, Shantarakshita will argue, is an unnecessary hypothesis.

The Introduction of Buddhism Into Tibet

Berkeley was puzzled about how an object, which he believed had mental but not physical reality, could remain in existence when no one was observing it. His solution was that it still exists in the mind of God. A parody of his answer is, given in the following limerick by Ronald Knox.[8]

There was a young man who said "God
Must think it exceedingly odd
If he finds that this tree
Continues to be
When there's no one about in the Quad"
(Reply)
Dear Sir:
Your astonishment's odd.
I am always about in the Quad
And that's why the tree
Contains to be,
Since observed by
Yours faithfully, God

But if there is no God to hold the mental world in existence, then we need a solution different from Berkeley's to account for the continuity of objects. Shantarakshita explains the apparent continuity in terms of mental objects. Kumarila and Subhagupta had argued that if there is a knower, there must be a thing known i.e. the external world. We know this world exists because of perception and inference and also from the fact that the world of our experience is by and large predictable.

The problem of apparent continuity of objects arises according to Shantarakshita from imagining the mind as a receptacle for forms (cognitions). But this is a false picture. Nor is the "knower" a producer of objects, conveniently producing the object of knowledge (2001) The preceding moment, as cause, is followed by a cognition which is that of "John seeing the tree." Whether or not this effect will come about depends not on John, nor on the external existence of the tree, but on whether or not the antecedent conditions were of such a nature as to be followed by the effect, John sees a tree. If John has had too many cocktails (a change in the antecedent conditions) he may see two trees. Thus one moment of consciousness produces the next with no need to posit the existence of the external world or the substantial (separate) existence of the cognizer.

Shantarakshita, of course, must be able to account for the distinction between appearance and reality (2053-2054). How can one say that Pema correctly sees one moon when sober and incorrectly sees two moons when drunk? Shantarakshita answers in the following way: "If.. .`being in conformity with reality' consists in being the cause of a cognition envisaging effective action, - then, this is possible also when the cognition is without an external objective basis. (2054)" What we seem to have here is a pragmatic theory of truth. The cognition of Pema that a horse is in front of him is "verified" if it is followed by certain other cognitions such that he is riding the horse. Usually this theory would work. In cases of extreme suggestibility or psychosis no test is possible for the individual. The madman will see the winged horse and believe he is riding away. On Shantarakshita's view can we say the madman is wrong if his chain of cognitions all work for him? Ultimately, one would guess that the answer is "no." Normality is a shared chain of cognitions, - -madness is a unique one. But on the grounds that the ego is unreal and the root of suffering, one could argue that a view of the world shared with the rest of humanity is better than one that is not. And as Shantarakshita says, the awareness of the Buddha is the best of all, for it is most productive of good effects being free from ego and the poisons.

This analysis of the nature of cognitions also illuminates another problem, the relation of agent to act. Briefly the argument runs: The doer of an action must persist through time. It must be there when the action is initiated and must persist in order to complete it. But since it has already been proved that all things are momentary, there is no agent. In the light of the discussion of cognition, one might say that the actor and the act both arise and disappear together, moment by moment, in the stream of experience.

In   Shantarakshita's study of philosophical questions, one is dramatically absent, -- free will. The pervasive nature of cause and effect seems to rule it out. Yet some aspects of the problem remain to be considered. Although everything on the relative level is consciousness, consciousness is not a unity. It has many forms. There are many different currents in the river. What appears to us as mind and what appears to us as matter have their own logic. The characteristic of the material realm is causal invariance. One drops a rock, - it falls. As Kamalashila says in his lengthy commentary to text 1886, "What is a fact is that when the modification of one thing always follows the modification of another, then alone can the one be regarded as the Material Cause of the other." By contrast, there is no such invariant concomitance between bodily states and subjective consciousness, nor between consciousness and action. For example (human actions) although caused by preceding subjective states are relatively free from physical causes. They are motivated by desires etc. which are the occasion for their arising. The behavior of the high bodhisattva which is free from desire is, nevertheless, not unmotivated. His or her action is motivated by the intention to benefit others. This intention, unlike desire is not compulsive, but rational, and not invariant concomitance. Such rational events are caused but not as strictly as our physical events.

Mahayanists believe, in a certain sense, since the bodhisattva has realized the absurdity of distinctions between self and other, his or her behavior becomes a manifestation of timeless wisdom and compassion. There are no temporal causes of this behavior. It just happens. Nor can the actions of the bodhisattva be supposed to be necessitated by non-intentional causal conditions. The way in which the bodhisattva manifests his or her compassion may be startingly unpredictable. As the stories of the siddhas indicate, it usually is.

Theory of Language

In chapter 16, Shantarakshita presents his theory of language which follows directly from his preceding analysis of experience. All of our experience consists in vijnana, -- there are no external objects. Words, therefore, cannot represent objects. How, then, is knowledge possible?

Let us take the word "cow". We have experiences that we call experiences of what is not a cow. "Cow" then, means all that which is not what are meant by other than cow. It is not an entity. It is a negation.(Shantarakshita follows the logicians Dignaga and Dharmakirti in this analysis.)

"This cow" couldn't refer to an entity because the word "cow" is used to mean cow at different times and since all is momentary, it would fail to refer twice to the same cow. Nor could it refer to a generality, for these, he has shown, are non-existent. Although not non-cow is logically equivalent to "cow", Shantarakshita is trying to avoid speaking in such a way as to imply reference to a distinct entity.

Further, this analysis makes it possible for Shantarakshita to account for our ability to speak meaningfully about unreal entities. (text 1112-1114) For example, there are no blue lotuses. But what we mean by the words "blue lotus" is anything which is not a non-lotus and not non-blue. If there doesn't happen to be any such thing, it doesn't matter. We are still able to say what it is not.

It is obvious that what is implied by this theory of language is a strict relativistic and conventional view of meaning. Words can only be understood in relation to other words.

Although Shantarakshita's position comes from Dignaga and Dharmakirti, it bears a striking resemblance to the view of the great sixth century Madhyamika philosopher Chandrakirti. Chandrakirti had insisted on the absolute conventionality of language. As Robert Thurman points out, it is this very insistence on conventionality of meaning that rules out nihilism. For while realizing the complete relativity of our experience we are nevertheless forced to think in conventional terms. we cannot abandon other human beings, responsibilities, pragmatic concerns, philosophical investigation itself. Our very mode of thinking is completed permeated with social reality.

Thurman cites a number of passages from Wittgenstein which highlight the extraordinary similarity between the view of the modern philosopher and Chandrakirti:[9]

"Wittgenstein is most explicit about the sheer conventionality of language, as in the following group of statements:

'The point here is not that our sense impressions can lie, but that we understand their language. (And this language, like any other is founded on convention.' (P.I. 355)

'One objects: "So you are saying that human agreement decides what is true and what is false?" -- It is what human beings *say* that is true and false; and they agree on the *language* they use. That is not agreement in opinions but in form of life.' (P.I. 241)

Here we strike rock bottom that is we have come down to conventions (P.I. 241)

'When philosophers use a word - "knowledge", "being", "object", "I", "proposition", "name" --and try to grasp the *essence of* the thing, one must always ask oneself: is this word ever actually used in this way in the language-game which is its original home. What *we* do is to bring the words back from their metaphysical to their everyday use.' (P.I. 116)

'The meaning of a word is its use in the language.' (P.I. 43)

'When I talk about language (words, sentences, etc.) I must speak the language of everyday. Is this language somehow too coarse and material for what we want to say? *Then how is another one to be constructed?'* (P.I. 120)

A main source of our failure to understand is that we do not command a clear view of the use of our words.' (P.I. 122)

Philosophy can in no way interfere with the actual use of language; it can in the end only describe it. For it cannot give it any foundation either. It leaves everything as it is.' (P.I. 124) *'Essence* is expressed by grammar.' (P.I. 371) 'Grammar tells us what kind of object everything is. I (P.I. 373) 8.

Shantarakshita and Chandrakirti do not seem to be in disagreement about the nature of the self. Both believe on the absolute level there is no self but on the level of conventional discourse it is all right to speak as if there were, and as long as one realizes the conventional nature of the designation it does not produce obstacles to enlightenment. Further, Shantarakshita is objecting to the view that the self is *unchanging.* Even on the conventional level he believes this to be false.[10]

Why do we call some things "cow" and not others? Shantarakshita answers this question in chapter 17 in terms of perception. When our experience takes a certain form , our awareness of this form produces knowledge. We know that it is different from other things and we give it a name. Perception is not the same as knowledge. When we perceive a pot there is a moment of experience that is free from awareness of form. Our first sight of a pot does not yield understanding of what it is. Perception, therefore, is not knowledge. Naive perception is free from error. (This is an important fact to understand in relation to his view of meditation).

What about the perceptions of enlightened beings? Shantarakshita discusses this problem in chapter 21, when he criticizes the view that entities remain the same throughout the past, present and future. The most important argument is a response to Vasumitra who argued that entities stay the same throughout the three aspects of time, but their relationships change. Their previous condition is called the past, now is called their present and their later condition is now called their future. just as a woman can be called a mother or a daughter depending on her relation to her father or to her son. Shantarakshita argues that for a thing to exist on the relative level it must be able to act (function as an efficient cause) or to be acted on. But the power of action exists only in the present. So no entity can exist in the past or future. (text 1842)

At the end of this chapter, Shantarakshita confronts a very interesting objection to the doctrine of the momentariness of entities. If the past and future do not exist, how can emancipated beings know them? The answer sheds a great deal of light on the manner in which the knowledge of an emancipated being is conceived.

The Mystics cognize that form of the 'Present' thing which directly or indirectly, has become either an effect, or a cause; subsequently, they follow it up with *conceptual cognitions,* which are purely common (secular) in character, and which are really without objects (without a real, objective background). Thus it is that, on the basis of the said past and future series of causes and effects, proceed all teachings regarding the Past and the Future. - As for the *Tathagata* Himself, His teachings proceed without circumlocution; because the Series of His cognitions are entirely devoid of the webs of Conceptual Context. (1853-1856)

Thus the enlightened meditation master does not actually see an existing future. Rather, consistent with the law of cause and effect and with momentariness, all that is claimed is that his or her insight into the present is so penetrating that the resulting inferences are much more accurate and refined than those of ordinary people. For example, about *The Sutra of the Wise and Foolish,* it is said that the foolish will understand it only as a funny, ironic story about reincarnation, but the wise will learn the lesson that if one wants to learn about one's previous lifetimes one must infer them from one's present situation.

The following analogy may be of use. A retarded child may not understand how someone may be able to say in winter that cherry trees will bloom in the spring. The person who says this is not viewing an already existing future. But rather, he or she knows the patterns of cherry trees. Similarly the enlightened being knows the "patterns" of things and in this sense knows the future. The analogy is limited because the situation of an omniscient being is different for such a person has transcended the illusion of individuality and is thus able to dwell in a state of non-conceptual wisdom. We cannot say what this is of course, but we can benefit from the compassionate manifestation of such a being.

The Tathagata's teaching proceeds without circumlocution because his nature has become like the Cintamani gem (wish fulfilling jewel) (text 3606-3610). To borrow a metaphor from Coleridge, the activity of the Tathagata is like the Aeolian harp, which plays when the wind blows. Because of the compassion of the Buddha his help spontaneously arises according to the need of beings without concept, inference or intention. In the last chapter Shantarakshita elaborates on the omniscience of the Buddha. The Tathagata, freed from all dualistic thinking, has transcended the distinction between mind and object, self

60

The Introduction of Buddhism Into Tibet

and other. Thus he is able to teach through all his surroundings,-- through the universe itself. Admitting there is no direct knowledge of an omniscient Buddha, such a being can be inferred. The Buddha, understanding the nature of reality, has destroyed the poisons and thus ignorance. These poisons produce all duality and conceptualization which are obstacles to wisdom. Therefore, when these are removed, omniscience should follow. Of course all beings who have achieved buddhahood are properly termed the Buddha.

The Buddha knows all things in a single cognition and in a single moment. (text 3627)This would follow from his transcendence of form i.e. conceptualization. For it is these forms which impel us to speak of things as having limits, of being x and non-x. Once form is transcended, there is no temporal element in awareness.

In his commentary to text 3627, Kamilashila mentions an interesting objection to the Buddha's omniscience, namely that it would generate the following paradox. One cannot know everything, because some things like space are limitless. If one were able to mentally encompass space, one' conception would necessarily be false. Kamilashila answers:

it is just because He (Buddha) does not apprehend things as *limited* that He becomes omniscient; otherwise, if He had apprehended the *limitless* things as *limited,* He would be clearly *mistaken.* Because one is called `omniscient' only when He apprehends *existing* things as *existent,* and *non-existing* things as *non-existent;*-and to the Region of *existence,* there is no limit at all. Hence if one apprehends as *non-existent* the limit which does *not exist* in the form of *movement,*-and if He apprehends as *existent,* the Limit, which does *exist* in the form of being cognised by the Omniscient Person,-why should He be regarded as `Not-Omniscient'?

These considerations concerning omnipotent buddhas may indeed seem a bit strange. But turning to the subject of ordinary perception, the problems are just as complex. To begin with, the object of thought must be a compound of objects, because the thought of an object is a result of several internal mental processes. The eye sees the color, the ear hears the sound, etc. The mind binds these experiences together and tells us that they all belong to the same object. (Even in terms of one sense, e.g. sight, we see different parts of an object successively. we see the head of a tall man, then his shoulders etc. But consciousness makes these things appear to us in such a way as if we were

61

experiencing them all at once.) The image of the tall man across the room enters our visual field as a tiny figure less than an inch in height. Yet our minds make the necessary changes for us, and we perceive such a person to be the same height he would be if he were directly in front of us. Perspective in other words, is automatically factored in for us. The object as we know it, is not an accurate representation of what we sense.

But if we assume that the parts of the object, the uncompounded objects, are the reality beneath the appearance we also run into trouble. Suppose we take the position that the objects of thought are atoms. As already pointed out, atoms are supposed to be indivisible elements. But anything which exists must have directions: to put it in terms relative to the earth, there is a north, south etc. But if atoms are simple and indivisible this cannot be. So how can atoms exist? If the atoms are empty in nature, how can objects be composed of them? Modern physics is also concerned with this problem. Atoms, even today, are considered so unpredictable and ephemeral in nature no one can explain how reality can be composed of them. There was an article in *Scientific American*, describing the work of a think tank at Stanford in which scientists were seriously considering the idea that elementary particles. ought not to be considered neither one nor many,--so reminiscent of Shantarakshita.[11]

What remains then, is our subjective knowledge of the world. But how can the external world and the subjective world be the same? Because one can know one's own experience directly, but not that of others. Descartes argued that the self can only know itself with certainty. Everything else is in doubt.

But Shantarakshita escapes the Cartesian dilemma because (as he argued in the early chapters of the *Tattvasamgraha)* the self is unreal. There really is no distinction between oneself and others. The inability to know the experience of others as well as our own is due to the six poisons. When these are removed one knows directly all of experience. And once subjective reality (consciousness) constitutes all of relative truth, one thus achieves omniscience. Of course all of this will have to be understood in a different way when the absolute point of view is introduced, but more of this later.

The effect follows the cause in an orderly, predictable way (e.g. plant a marigold seed in good soil with light and water and you get a marigold) because both "cause" and "effect" originate from consciousness. Of course they do not originate in most cases from the individual consciousness alone. If that were the case we could make wine out of water. Sometimes the individual consciousness does function as cause as, for example, when we write a poem. But cases such as the marigold seed producing the marigold come from the ocean of consciousness which Shantarakshita calls vijnana.

Ego-clinging distorts the vijnana and produces a stream of consciousness immersed in suffering. Liberated consciousness sees itself as one with the totality, and being selfless, does not suffer. Although Shantarakshita does not say this we might speculate that if reality is composed of mostly enlightened minds we would have a paradise and if mainly unenlightened minds, a hell. One might rightly object that if the vijnana is itself momentary, it *cannot* explain invariant concomitance. Why does one mental moment bring about the next in an orderly way? Why is the suffering consciousness of a bereaved lover at time (1) followed by suffering consciousness of this lover at time (2)? Why couldn't it just as well be followed by joy? To explain it by karma would beg the question because karma is just a form of causality. Shantarakshita does not give us an answer to this question. All states, psychic and physical plant their seeds at one moment and the results are reaped the next, in an orderly way.

The *Madhyamakalankara*

Let us now return to the *Madhyamakalankara*. The argument proceeds two ways. The incoherence of the concept of an external (non-mental) object, either compounded or uncompounded, is demonstrated. Consciousness is left as the only alternative, and the substantial non-duality of subject and object once shown to be feasible, leaves consciousness in possession of the field, at least on the relative level. On the absolute level, which is free from the concept of one or many, subject-object.one cannot even say reality is mind (consciousness). In this way Shantarakshita unifies the views of Nagarjuna and Asanga.

Shantarakshita begins by arguing that nothing can be permanent. He means this in the strong sense that everything is momentary. Each moment of time seems to be connected with the next as its cause. Yet only one moment exists at a time. It follows that each point in the causal process is instantaneous. So they cannot really be connected. Shantarakshita follows Nagarjuna on this point.

He agrees with Vasubandhu's critique of atomism:

> Nor can the atomic theory be true. For if atoms are not connected with each other, they cannot form the elements. But even if they are connected with each other, they are not indivisible (partless). (11-14)
>
> Self consciousness can be said to be indivisible. It cannot be divided into subject and object. Thus it cannot know itself as object. For consciousness is pure subjectivity. (18)

But what is the nature of consciousness, and what are its objects? Shantarakshita argues:

> The objects of consciousness are not external to the mind. They are but reflections of it. For we can only know what our minds tell us. "One can never see the external object" *(per se).* (21)
>
> Further a single thought can't be divided. (If one thinks of a dozen eggs, one's thought can't be divided into twelve). But then, if my thought is an indivisible unity, how can it represent a manifold? Thus thought is not a representation of external objects. (22-23)

Shantarakshita considers the view that cognitions arise gradually but so quickly we mistakenly think they happen all at once. When one sees a black bird, for example, one first knows it is black, has a yellow beak, is a bird etc. If this were the case, i.e. if one perceived successively, so quickly, but not simultaneously, one wouldn't know if what was heard was lata (vine) or tala (fan palm). (24-26) But we can distinguish the order of sounds.

Shantarakshita replies that the mind jumps from one thought to another. One thinks, say, of a chocolate bar, then, immediately after, the shop where one can buy one. If one thought about things one aspect at a time, the mind would not jump about this way. "All the different aspects of the object are captured instantaneously by perception." (27)

Nor can one argue that some things that seem instantaneous are really gradual, as a torch whizzed about appears as a circle. One can only perceive what is in the present. One doesn't perceive the circle but infers it through memory. (28-30) But the torch too, is a concept based on perception, not perceived as torch.

Some argue there are many minds involved in each act of perception. Each aspect of an external object is known by a separate mind. Shantarakshita argues that this cannot be because objects can be divided endlessly. Is each of these parts known by a separate mind? And how could this be the case when these parts are so small as to be imperceptible? (31-33) Nor can the mind involved in an act of perception be a unity. If it were indivisible it would be unchangeable and would not be able to relate to a changing world.

Some realist philosophers had argued that one of the elements, (earth, or air etc.) was the only substance. But these philosophers had also claimed that direct perception was the only veridical knowledge. Their view is inconsistent because one cannot know through direct perception that all is air, or fire etc. (37)

Nor can it be consistently argued as it was with the Samkhyas, that the three qualities (brightness, force, mass) are reducible to the single principle of nature. For if nature is one, it cannot be manifested as many, or inconsistency would be an essential part of reality, and we could never know it. (Idealists such as the Advaita (Monistic) Vedantists and the idealist Buddhists argued that since matter is an incoherent concept, all must come from mind. And since all distinctions are imaginary, mind must be one. All that occurs is a result of the maturing habits or tendencies of this mind.

But according to Shantarakshita, mind cannot be one, because what it knows is many, and if subject and object are identical, and objects are manifold, so is mind. Some argue that the distinct objects are not real. They are magical illusions. Shantarakshita replies that if they were not really distinct, we couldn't learn about events sequentially. We would learn everything all at once. For temporal divisions imply disunity. Not even a magic trick can fake this. (44) Even if reality were really one, our names for it are distinct. And these names are made up of letters. So we do know at least that these are distinct objects.

Yet it is generally correct that, although mind is a manifold, we do know what appears to our minds (sense impressions) rather than external objects. Shantarakshita then considers the view that these objects, though mental, are real (rnam bden pa). There are three forms of this view.

(a) Some have argued that there are two aspects to mind (half egg theory). Although from the absolute point of view (pure consciousness) all is one mind, from the relative point of view, there are minds and distinct objects. Like a split hard-boiled egg, at each perception is half mind, half-object. Shantarakshita rejects this, because it is a contradiction to say that the same mind can be both one and many. And in addition, if mind on the absolute level is an absolute unity, it cannot manifest itself as a diversity. If this were the case, all opposites, moving, not moving, before, after, would be the same, which would be very hard to accept as true. (46-48) Further, these philosophers believe we perceive one aspect of a thing at a time. But this cannot account for the fact that we can perceive some things to be hot and others to be cold simultaneously.

(b) Shantarakshita considers another form of idealism held by some Buddhists, namely that each person has many minds knowing many mental objects. If, as Buddhists, they have rejected the idea of an unchanging mind, then there is a separate mind for each individual at every instant. And everything that exists must be held in existence by a separate act of consciousness. So there would have to be a separate mind (thought) for each of these. But we are aware of no such thing. (49)

(c) Some believe that distinct objects are just a reflection of one continuous mind; objects are perceived to be different, but really of a single nature. But if this were the case we would have no explanation for why distinctions arose in the first place.

d) Some believe that there really are no objects, - not even mental ones (rnam rdzun pa), the perception of objects is a mistake. But this is contrary to common sense. What we call mental has quite different qualities from what we call physical. Further, things certainly appear to be different from each other. Mental states, for example, such as happiness and unhappiness are not the same. Are all these distinctions an illusion? If this were the case we could not know anything at all. For if something is an object of knowledge it must be directly perceived, -- even internal states such as pain are perceived in this way. But if something doesn't exist at all, it can't be perceived.

How all forms of idealism fail

If there is nothing but mind, how can awareness of, objects arise in the mind? This must be caused and so the causal conditions which produce awareness in the individual `mind" must exist apart from that mind. Otherwise it would have no experience. It is dependent for experience on causal conditions.(60)

As a result of this investigation Shantarakshita concludes that all things, including the individual mind are dependent on other things. (inter-dependent co-origination) . Nothing can exist independently of other things. Not even the individual mind is self-sufficient.

So we know things, he concludes, in an artificial way. We seem to know them as independent things, -- chairs, tables, etc. But on closer examination we see this is impossible. our awareness is held in existence by interdependent causal conditions which are beyond our ken. We only see the result - like a mirage. We see the chair and the table but not their real nature. The very notion of existence and non-existence is a category imposed by the mind. Ultimate reality admits of no distinctions, of no theories etc. We can say nothing about it. Thus holding no theory, Shantarakshita places himself above criticism. (67-71)

At this point Shantarakshita changes his approach. Having argued that reality is beyond conception, he raises the question as to why people can't directly perceive it non-conceptually. He concludes that it must be because consciousness is obscured by habits of categorization and evaluation, --tendencies due to karma and environment. (73-74) So what hope is there that anyone will attain absolute awareness? Shantarakshita claims this is possible through the attainment of yogic perception through meditation. (75) This is possible because the absolute and relative levels are ways of intuiting the same reality, -- one pure, one impure. Reason can show the necessity of going beyond ordinary knowledge because it can show that ordinary knowledge is confused. Similarly, sense experience, purified, leads, through yogic meditation, to pure awareness.

The relative level, then is of great value, it is not to be rejected. If, on the relative level, one removes the causal conditions producing obscurations, the obscurations will disappear and the true nature will be attained. (82-87)

So the idealists are correct to argue that the relative level has the nature of mind. (91) However, one can see that phenomena including mind have no independent reality. This shows the Madhyamikas are right that the ultimate nature of reality is emptiness.

Are subject and object the same or different?

There seems to be a contradiction between what Shantarakshita says in the *Tattvasamgraha* and the *Madhyamakalankara* about the duality or non-duality of mind and object. In the *Tattvasamgraha* he argues against those who say there must be a separate unchanging self who is the knower of the object. Among his many arguments against this view is the infinite regress charge that to know the substantial self demands another knower, and so on. But in the *Madhyamakalankara* he argues that subject and object cannot be the same because a subject is that which knows. It can never be an object. Subject and object like hot and cold demand each other. For reasons of non-vacuous contrast they must be distinguishable.

So what is Shantarakshita's view about the relation between subject and object? An analogy with the dancer and the dance may be helpful. The dancer and the dance are *distinguishable* but not *inseparable.* The self is not a *thing* existing apart from its object. But it is distinguishable from the object in many ways determined by context; by the situations in which the personal pronoun "I" is used. This does not mean that the "I" is unchanging. The dancer changes along with the dance.

Since the objects of knowledge are all mental in nature, on the relative level, subject and object can be said to be equally mental. For surely the subject is as mental as anything can be. So on the relative level, Shantarakshita is an idealist. But on the absolute level idealism itself is inadequate, for mind itself, being a concept, cannot be non-relativistically real.

There are, therefore, two levels of relative truth. On the rough, everyday common sense level, there are knowers and objects of knowledge. These appear to be separable, but on closer examination objects are discovered to be forms of thought. Only on the absolute level is thought itself discovered to be empty in nature

As summarized in Ven. Khenchen Palden Sherab Rinpoche's commentariy on the *Madhyamakalankara:*

A) Relative Level (Unanalyzed)

On this level it is correct to make distinctions between real and unreal, hot and cold, table and chair, large objects and atoms etc. These concepts form a network of meaning in which each term depends on others for its usefulness to us.

B) Relative Level (Analyzed)

When we examine external reality closely, we discover that terms like atom, matter, elements, make no sense. Nor does the notion of a single element such as nature make sense. But internal reality is in no better shape. The notion of one mind is incoherent; but so is the notion of many minds.

It is also impossible to maintain that the mind depends on nothing else. If this were the case we could not account for the orderly arising of thoughts. So there is interdependent co-origination. Mind depends on this.

Nor is it possible to deny awareness. To do so is self contradictory, because there must be awareness to deny awareness. So on the Pure Relative Level, one can assert the reality of awareness and interdependent co-origination.

C) Impure Ultimate Level

On closer examination, however, we discover two truths:

1) Given Nagarjuna's critique of causality, inter-dependent co-origination is itself an incoherent concept.

2) Given the fact that awareness is pure subjectivity, it can never be known directly as an object. So it is unknowable.

D) Pure Absolute Truth

Reality is beyond conception. We call it emptiness.

At this point Shantarakshita would seem to have ascended from the analysis of idealist positions with respect to the relative level of conceptual experience, showing that each idealist view leads to inconsistencies. A explanation of these inconsistencies must take us outside the relative level. In suggesting that the causes of our perceptions cannot lie within the field of experience, he seems to contradict his Humean definition of causality as invariant concomitance between observed classes of events. For the causes of perception are not themselves perceptible.

There are two possible escapes from this paradox. Either "cause" is being used in a new and special sense, or else he is only suggesting that reason impels us to look for causes in a direction in which they cannot actually be found. The second view is similar to Kant's explanation of the noumenal as a regulative principle, rather than an object of possible knowledge.

Near the end of the *Madhyamakalankara*, Shantarakshita faces the paradox of skepticism. On the absolute level, he wants to maintain that nothing can be known as true. But how can he express this without asserting a fact about knowledge? He does so by refusing to assert anything as true. Therefore there is nothing for anyone to refute.(68)

Shantarakshita has not rejected ordinary truth on the functional (pragmatic) level:

On the relative level, I did not reject
Either the relations of cause and effect between entities
Or categories of samsara and nirvana etc.
These concepts should not be mixed up on the relative level.
Since we can clasify things in terms of cause and effect,

And characterize phenomena in general on the relative level,
The accumulation path can exist in a pure state.
Thus from the point of view of the middle way all phenomena are
useful. (84,85)
And useful in gaining enlightenment, for,
By means of a completely pure cause
A completely pure effect arises. (86)

At this point I will defer to Ven. Khenchen Palden Sherab
Rinpoche's excellent commentary:

Starting with verse sixty-three, he puts aside his discussion of
the absolute level and turns his attention to the relative. The
relative level has three main characteristics. It seduces the mind
into accepting reality, because 1) on the unexamined level it looks
perfectly convincing. 2) It is constantly changing, as instant by
instant it disappears and is replaced by the arising of the next
instant. Nothing is permanent,--phenomena are an endless stream
of birth and death. All that exists is functional,--that is, anything
real functions as a cause in the system of interdependent co-
origination. This stream of causes stretches endlessly into the
future. Every result comes about in this way, relying on causes
immediately before it.

There is, therefore, no permanent cause. Some argue that
Ishvara is a permanent cause. But what reason have they for their
view? No one has ever found a permanent cause.

So that is all you can say about the relative level,--that is, that
it is constantly changing in accordance with cause and effect, and
when you analyze even this, you find its nature is emptiness.
Other than this, Shantarakshita has no opinion about it. So there is
nothing to refute in his system. For it rests squarely on the
ultimate level. And on the ultimate level, existence and non-
existence are categories which do not apply, for this level is
beyond distinctions...."[12]

In verse 70, (Shantarakshita) forestalls a possible criticism that
he can say nothing about the absolute level at all, since it is beyond
conception. He points out that there is nevertheless some
similarity between what he says and the absolute level, because the
absolute level is beyond distinctions and complexities, and his
method of reasoning breaks down distinctions and complexities.
Further, there are two levels of the absolute, one of which is

accessible in accordance with the capabilities of ordinary people. One of these ordinary ways to the absolute is through reasoning,-- another way lies through selfless virtue and devotion. The only way to the higher absolute level is beyond ordinary capabilities, for it involves the spontaneous opening of the wisdom mind.

The *Tattvasiddhi*

The *Tattvasamgraha* and *Madhvamakalankara* are philosophical masterpieces on the level of relative truth. In the *Tattvasiddhi,* Shantarakshita explains how the tantra leads to the absolute level. His argument unfolds in terms of ethics and logic.

The central issue which Shantarakshita confronts is the Theravada (Hinayana) and Mahayana teachings that desires are defilements and obstacles to enlightenment. Shantarakshita does not deny the truth of this teaching on the ordinary level. But he argues that a realized person, because of his or her egolessness, can transform the poison of desire and attachment into the nectar of liberation. He also argues that this is not contrary to the teachings of the Buddha who is quoted in *The Heap of Jewels Sutra* as having said that the rubbish of the city can be used as manure in the sugar cane and grape fields. What justification does Shantarakshita offer for this position?

His argument follows directly from his metaphysical theory which he presented in the *Tattvasamgraha* and the *Madhyamakalankara.* It is the mind which imposes form and categories on reality. The most pernicious of these forms are the categories of self and other. The idea of self, produced through ignorance, gives rise to the other poisons of anger, hatred, greed, jealousy and fear. These distort our vision of reality and poison our world. If this process is reversed, by tantric practice involving mantra and mudra, the poisonous aspect of experience is eliminated. But this purified response to experience does more than just eliminate poison. It allows us to achieve awareness on the absolute level.

Let us go back to our central analogy for understanding tantra, the relation between aesthetic experience and ordinary experience. Imagine a painter, perhaps Ingres, who is entranced with the beauty of the female body. His appreciation is both sensual and loving. He does not see it as a symbol, (of God for example), but as beautiful, quite heavenly, in its own nature. Such a painter in his day horrified and frightened ordinary people who saw in his enraptured acceptance of erotic sensuality an invitation to a low form of unbridled lust and the cruelty which often accompanies it. But now most educated people realize that Ingres' appreciation of the nude body was aesthetic rather than a mere desire for a sexual release. This does not mean that Ingres necessarily did not feel sexual passion as he painted his models. It means rather that this passion was transformed into a vision of the aesthetic qualities of the figure as well as a sharing of his experience with those of his audience capable of aesthetic response.

To repeat a point made earlier, aesthetic qualities are linked to but not reducible to other types of qualities such as physical qualities. An example is balance in a painting. A balanced painting evokes in us a feeling somewhat akin to seeing a dancer balancing *en pointe*, or, more prosaically, a construction worker balancing on a beam. But balance in a painting transcends the physical origins of the meaning of the word. It is also non-reducible in terms of the elements of the painting itself. For example symmetry may produce balance or its opposite. It depends on the use of color, perspective, even subject matter. Aesthetic qualities may even depend on the context in which the work of art is placed. If a simple box-like structure is placed in a concentration camp it may appear quite different than if placed in a garden.

The enlightened person has realized his or her oneness with all things, and in a timeless way. So there need not be any clinging or attachment of any kind to any part of experience. All is enjoyed in a state of equanimity. And compassion spontaneously arises in the form of activity designed to share this bliss with all beings.

We can understand the difficulty the great teachers have in explaining this mode of experience to ordinary people if we consider how difficult it would be to explain aesthetic experience to someone completely devoid of it. Aesthetic awareness is a higher perspective on life, -- to understand it one must share it. Fortunately most, perhaps all human beings have some understanding of such aesthetic qualities as beauty, grace, vitality etc. Through study and experience such perception is enhanced. Vajrayana Buddhists believe that all sentient beings have at least a dim awareness of their own enlightened nature. This seed of enlightenment is called the tathatagarbha. So through study and experience they can be led to an appreciation of the true nature in a way analogous to how someone can deepen their appreciation of art. Or they may "recover their aesthetic sight" as someone with hysterical blindness can be cured.

To return now to the analysis of mantra and mudra, Shantarakshita says in the *Tattvasiddhi* that these are the means of achieving the transformation of experience from the level of the ordinary to that of realization. There are particular mantras and mudras which are designed to heighten awareness. Because of their special qualities, they are able to help people to see all of experience as mudra and mantra; i.e. as manifestations of wisdom/ emptiness/ skillful means. For example the mudra of the open hand of generosity can, combined with a sense of egolessness, induce in us a feeling as if being itself were generous. The mantra spoken with devotion and a sense of formlessness, opens one to the feeling that all sounds are the sounds of the Buddha. In this way experience is raised to a higher perspective as the fruit of a sour fruit tree, which has been grown from seeds soaked in milk, becomes sweet.

One might argue that the heightening of experience can be done more safely within the realm of monastic discipline. Why does the tantric practitioner have to become involved with such apparently troublesome aspects of experience as desire and furious wrathful deities? But would it not be shortsighted to tell a great painter or playwright to look only at the pretty side of life and ignore the rest? If an artist were to follow such a foolish course, how could he or she bring about the aesthetic transformation of the tragic and ugly side of life? Similarly if duality is to be overcome, all of life must be embraced and transformed. There are no exceptions. And the difficult, disgusting and horrible are challenges to the Tantrayana practitioner. Such a view is not unique to Buddhism. In their great compassion some Christian saints embraced lepers only to find themselves embracing the body of Christ.

The bodhisattva wishes for the unexcelled happiness of all beings. But such happiness cannot possibly be achieved through penance, - through the bodhisattva's self-torment. Only through happiness and gladness can one achieve Buddhahood. (Folio 56)

This absolute nature cannot be described in words, but because it is experienced as perfect bliss, it is not completely incorrect to describe its nature as the union of wisdom and compassion. For this bliss never ends, never harms, never diminishes.

By the process of transformation of perception the yogi can use the world of forms to produce great happiness. Just as an object cannot be both hot and cold at the same time and in the same way, so a being cannot at the same time be both completely happy and unhappy. Through one's practice, that is through the combination of meditation (wisdom/emptiness) and compassion skillful means) one can become completely and unchangingly happy:

73

The Introduction of Buddhism Into Tibet
Striving diligently for bodhichitta, how should the yogi achieve this transformation? By abandoning the ego completely. And not through the torments of asceticism. How else but through bliss will one attain bliss? (Folio 56)

Why is this the case? This is because the bodhisattva's mind has become naturally luminous.This luminosity arises from non-attachment to form. Where there is no attachment to form, there can be no suffering. The mind on the absolute level is in a state of equanimity no matter what circumstances arise. In the Theravada and Mahayana traditions, this detachment is achieved through duality or opposites. The antidote for illusion is meditation on dependent arising. The antidote for lust is meditation on the repulsiveness of the human body. In Vajrayana, however, one achieves detachment through desires. Or, to put it another way, through the practice of skillful means and wisdom. The bodhisattva uses the world of forms to go beyond both attachment and non-attachment:

> Sentient beings, having been brought into the great path, must understand that many different causes in combination bring about (different) results. Thus the cause of knowledge of egolessness will result in a person never being burdened with attachments. There is no other way to gain this great happiness. Because of this food, all activities will be transformrd into great bliss. Because do not people become similar to what possesses them? How in any other manner could a person become transformed?(Folio 56)

Although many methods for doing this are employed in the Vajrayana, the most powerful is the mudra of touch. Through the pleasure experienced in this way, one loses attachment to everything else. But as this equanimity itself is experienced on a higher and higher level it becomes transformed into an experience of absolute non-duality; oneness with being itself. In this way, attachment even to the object of touching is transcended.

When the madalunga (thorn apple) seed is dyed by the fruit of the laksa (a kind of. citron), then its fruit becomes similar to laksa. So when the mind has achieved liberation through bliss it can only dwell in bliss.

1. Ven Khenpo Tsewang Dongayal Rinpoche ibid.

2.

2.Shantarakshita *The Tattvasamgraha* trans. Ganganatha Jha vol. 1 & 2 Delhi: Motilal Banarsidass, 1986

3.Shantarakshita *Madhyamakalamkara* trans. Ven. Khenchen Palden Sherab Rinpoche and Ven. Khenpo Tsewang Dongyal Rinpoche forthcoming Boca Raton: Skydancer Press)

4. Lopez, Donald *Svatantrika* Ithaca: Snow Lion Press, 1987, p. 233

5. Ibid. p. 56

6. Descartes, Rene' *Principles of Philosophy* trans. Miller, V.R. and Miller, R.P. London: Reidel, 1983 p. 11
Descartes embraces the paradoxical view of momentary causality criticized by Shantarakshita, attempting to solve it by introducing a God that keeps the universe from going out of existence.

7. Ramanuja *Vedanta Sutras,* trans. Thibault, George , Delhi: Motilal Banarsidass, 1966 pp. 161-174

8. Knox, Ronald quoted in Abelson, R., Friquegnon, M., and Lockwood M., op. cit., p. 89

9. Thurman, Robert *The Central Philosophy of Tibet: A Study and Translation of Jey Tsong Khapa's Essence of True Eloquence* Princeton: Princeton University Press, 1984 pp. 99-100

10. "Yet even though it is all right to speak on the conventional level as if there were a self, (one can say I ate an apple), nevertheless, both Chandrakirti and Shantarakshita agree that even on the conventional level there is no self " Lopez op. cit.

11. Madhusree, Mukerjee "Explaining Everything" *Scientific American* January, 1996 p. 88

12. Ven. Khenchen Palden Sherab Rinpoche op. cit.

3

Shantarakshita, Shankara and the Problem of Nihilism

Sometime within the sixth and eighth century, Buddhist philosopher Shantarakshita and the Vedantin Shankara lived and worked. They do not seem to have debated with each other. (Shantarakshita mentions a Shankara in *Tattvasamgraha* (3206), but it is not the famous Vedantin. In 3554 comm., Kamilashila identifies this Shankara with the god Shiva.)

If they had met, they could have entered into a dialogue that would have been extremely fruitful for inter-religious understanding. Shantarakshita says nothing negative about Advaita Vedanta the school associated with Shankara, except that they make a slight mistake, that is 1) think that the Absolute Brahman can be one and permanent and yet assume many forms and 2) that all things can be a form of god while beings are still in need of liberation.

Shankara, however, has many criticisms of the Buddhists. 1) He argues that the Buddhists claim that the Buddha taught contradictory and false philosophies namely that a) the external world was real (Theravada) b) all things are composed of mind (Yogachara-Chittamatra) and c) all things are empty in nature. (Madhyamika) 2)

Shankara and the Problem of Nihilism
Buddhists are nihilistic, and nihilism cannot be used as a guide to life.
3) Buddhists do not accept an eternal unchangeable reality which forms
the basis of the world of appearance. Shankara rejects the momentary
collective unconscious or alaya of the Yogacharas as an adequate
foundation for phenomena.[1]

What might Shantarakshita have said in reply to Shankara? First of
all, being famous for his cheerfulness, gentleness and conciliatory
manner, he would have told Shankara about their points of agreement.
He would have been particularly delighted by four of Shankara's views,
1) that one must distinguish between the Absolute level which is
ineffable,-- beyond categories and concepts - and the relative level, 2)
that language about the Absolute is directional. It is not literally true of
the Absolute, but functions as a finger pointing at the moon. One must
not mistake the finger of language for the moon of the true nature. 3)
that, as Gaudapada, Shankara's paramaguru, (highest teacher) put it,
grasping must be completely eliminated in order that enlightenment
can be reached.[2] And 4) that the individual self is insubstantial.

To defend Buddhism against Shankara's charges, Shantaraksita
would probably have argued in the following way: 1) The Buddha did
not really teach in contradictory ways. All of the Buddha's teaching can
be understood as a series of finer and finer distinctions concerning the
means needed for the elimination of craving. I will now give a rather
lengthy discussion of how this historical development is said to have
occurred.

Buddhists who adhere to the "second and third turning of the
wheel," that is, the Mahayana and the Vajrayana, argue that the Buddha
taught in such a way that what he said could be understood in simple
terms by his early followers and yet serve as the source of more
sophisticated philosophical conclusions in later years. (Similar claims
were to be made by Christians about what Christ said to his disciples.)
The basic cure for human suffering in all three vehicles, however, was
believed to be the elimination of grasping. Without consciousness,
there is no suffering. But to eliminate consciousness is to cease to live
and although there would then be no suffering, this would be "throwing
the baby out with the bath water." It is only the craving part of
consciousness that causes suffering and hence must go.

As I have said, the history of Buddhism is really the development
of how to find more and more subtle ways of eliminating craving.
From the very beginning, the source of this craving was identified as
the belief in the substantial nature of the individual self.
Philosophically, the argument was stated very early in *The Questions of*

*King Milinda.*3 Just as the word "chariot: does not stand for a separate entity, but only for a collection of parts such as the axle and wheels, so the name, Nagasena, does not stand for a separate entity. It is the name of a collection of skandhas or bundles such as a certain series of thoughts, acts of will, sensations, bodily parts and consciousness. One cannot "store up treasure" for such a self for it is never "itself," but constantly changes as its parts change. Once one has eliminated all self-oriented desires, one achieves peace and suffering is at an end. This is the joy of Nirvana.

As discussed before many early Buddhists, such as the Vaibaishikas, (Shankara calls them Sarvastivadins) believed that the external world was composed of atoms, and that these were the real objects of our knowledge. Others, such as the Sautrantikas, believed that while atoms were real their nature was beyond conception. For we never know atoms, which are colorless, tasteless etc., but only sense impressions. But these impressions are caused by atoms.

Madhyamika philosophers such as Nagarjuna, believed that the elimination of craving involved not just clinging to luxuries and loved ones, health and sensual pleasure, but also clinging to one's favorite philosophical point of view. I suppose Nagarjuna, who was surrounded by intellectuals, realized how strong attachments to theories could be. How useful to show no one could hold a theory about anything!

Nagarjuna's main reason for generating his paradoxes however, was undoubtedly to break down the belief in the existence of objects, because if one does not believe in their non-relative (ultimate) existence it is harder to cling to them. It is interesting to note Gaudapada's insistence on the same point.3.

Nagarjuna's arguments unfold in a manner reminiscent of Zeno's paradoxes. They are directed particularly against the ultimate reality of the world of appearances and the intelligibility of causal relations.

When Nagarjuna first taught in this way, he encountered quite a bit of opposition. He was accused of nihilism, and 'of denying the central thesis of Buddhism, that is, that suffering is caused by craving. To this he replied in the following way: Reality is beyond our conception. But it appears to us relativistically. Buddha taught on a relative level. There was no other way. But his teaching was designed to lift us above that level. We do this through the elimination of craving. To eliminate craving, however, we must no longer cling to the relative level. We use the teaching as a ladder. When we have reached where we are going, we will throw the ladder away.

But Nirvana (the absolute) and Samsara (the relative) are not separate realms. They are distinguishable in the sense that Nirvana is beyond our relativistic conception. They are not different entities.

XXI   "Insoluble "are antinomic' views
Regarding what exists beyond Nirvana,
Regarding what the end of this would is,
Regarding its beginning ...

XXIII What is identity, and what is difference?
What is difference?
What is eternity, what non-eternity?
What means eternity and non-eternity together?
What means negation of both issues?

XXIV The bliss consists in the cessation of all thought,
In the quiescence of plurality.
No (separate) reality was preached at all,
Nowhere and none by Buddha! 4.

This is the philosophical statement of what is said in the *Heart Sutra* of the *Prajanaparamita* where it is proclaimed that "form is emptiness" and "emptiness is form". This view of Nagarjuna's is criticized as nihilistic by Shankara under the name of Sunyavadin or "emptiness" Buddhism. I will return later to the charge of nihilism, but now I wish to explain the charges directed against the Yogachara on what Shankara calls the Vijnavada school.

For Buddhists, everything on the relative level is momentary. (Strictly speaking, the absolute level is neither permanent nor momentary). Mahayana Buddhists, who followed Nagarjuna in denying the reality of atoms, were perplexed about a problem (discussed by Berkeley in the west) about how, if we know everything in terms of our own mental conceptions, we agree from one person to another about what it is we perceive. Jane and John, for example, will both see a cat in front of them.

This problem was taken up in the fourth century by two brothers, Vasubandhu and Asanga. Rejecting materialism, they believed subject and object were both products of ever changing momentary states of consciousness. Since there was no entity-the self, subject and object were part of the same flow. For Shantarakshita, subject and object were nevertheless distinguishable but not inseparable, like waves in the

Shankara and the Problem of Nihilism

ocean of mind (alaya). Shantarakshita argues for a kind of conceptual dualism on the relative level, for the subject is just that which can never become object. If it did so, it would have to be known by another object which would entail an infinite regress.

Some momentary states of consciousness produce in the various skandhas which we call persons, similar experiences because they are produced by similar causal conditions. It is these alaya, or momentary states of consciousness, which Shankara argues are an inadequate foundation for reality.

Asanga and Vasubandhu however, probably believed that the alaya is only a useful explanatory tool at the relative level, because consciousness is a concept that can be contrasted with non-consciousness, and since at the absolute level all concepts and distinctions are non-applicable, one could only conclude that the nature of the alaya is itself emptiness.

It is this latter position that is endorsed by Shantarakshita in the *Madhyamakalankara.* He speaks of himself as riding a chariot holding the bridles of two horses, the Madhyamika and the Yogachara (Sunyavada and Vijnavada). The Yogachara philosophy is generally true on the relative level, but on closer examination, can be shown to be unintelligible. (His criticisms of the Yogachara philosophy in the *Madhyamakalankara* analyzed earlier, are very close to Shankara's criticisms of that school. I will return to this later.) In the spirit of the development of Buddhist philosophy, Shantarakshita is saying that even clinging to consciousness as real is an obstacle to enlightenment.

2) Let us now return to Shankara's claim that Buddhism is nihilistic and cannot be a guide to life. First a brief discussion to put the subject in its historical context.

Buddhists commonly refer to Buddhism as "The Middle Way", that is, the way between eternalism and nihilism. By eternalism, they mean the belief that there are eternal, unchanging substances. By rejecting nihilism, they meant not only to reject the view that there is nothing whatever, but also to distinguish themselves from groups like the Charvakas who were moral as well as metaphysical nihilists. They were also considered to have lived morally reprehensible lives, but they may have had a bad press.

Buddhists, on the other hand, believed in reincarnation, correct moral behavior, religious practices such as prayer and meditation, and what can be loosely called "the sacred". Shankara would question whether or not they had a right to this religious form of life given their philosophy. Shantarakshita would say that on the absolute level he has

81

no philosophy. But on the experiential level, he is convinced that the elimination of craving leads not to a negative or neutral state, but to a state of perfect fulfillment, absolute bliss, the awareness of which is expressed on the relative level through a life of wisdom and compassion.

Shantarakshita discusses this experiential awakening in the *Tattvasiddhi*. Since enlightenment does not exist in a separate realm from samsara, it is possible to use cause and effect to alter the mind in such away that enlightenment happens. Shantarakshita says that just as the seed of a certain bitter fruit can be soaked in milk before planting to produce sweet fruit, so it is possible to use special religious practices to unravel our conceptual awareness and reveal the true nature of non-conceptual awareness. And it just happens to be the case that the true or absolute nature is perceived by the enlightened mind in such a way that the ideas of bliss, wisdom and compassion do not seem totally inappropriate in describing it. This does not seem to be a nihilistic ending of a religious quest. Emptiness is not nothing. 'It' is full of qualities, but these are beyond conception.

The way to the attainment of suchness, among other practices, is living one's life in terms of compassion, loving kindness, and joy in the joy of others. This is not just Shantarakshita's view but was generally accepted by Buddhists. This not only breaks down craving and all forms of selfishness but also the distinction between self and others. With the awareness of the true nature, this attitude is maintained effortlessly. Something about the awareness of the absolute is said to make selfless activities spontaneous. So the philosophy of emptiness can be said to be a guide for life.

Shankara had claimed that the momentary alaya was an inadequate foundation for reality. As we have already seen, Shantarakshita would agree with him. In the *Madhyamalankara* he gives arguments designed to show that whether one says that the mental subject or mental object are one or many, one runs into insurmountable difficulties. On the other hand, he would reject Shankara's criticism of the alaya, namely that an unchanging cognizer is needed to account for daily activities like memory or recognition which are subject to residual impressions dependent on place, time and cause. The counter argument would be that to assume they *are* the memories of an enduring person would be to beg the question and that similarity of the causal conditions from one moment to the next would be sufficient to generate the illusion that they belong to an enduring self.

Nevertheless, the two philosophers agree with the conclusion that the mind cannot be ultimately real. It is not the foundation of reality. Let us reverse the direction of our investigation at this point, and ask how Shankara might reply to Shantarakshita's criticisms of the advaita point of view.

1) Can Brahman be one and permanent yet assume many forms? Shantarakshita would say no. But was Shantarakshita replying to an Advaita philosophy that accepted the distinction between the relative and absolute as did Shankara's? Perhaps not. Let us return to the Buddhist distinction between the absolute and the relative. Concepts and distinctions can only be applied on the relative level. The relative level is momentary. But the four-fold negation applies on the absolute level, so strictly speaking, the absolute level is neither permanent, nor changing, nor permanent and changing, nor neither permanent nor changing.

But Shankara also claims that words have only a directional use when applied to the Absolute. They cannot be applied literally to the ineffable. So how can the words `permanent' and 'self' be correctly applied? Does Shankara wish this to mean any more than that in some way the sacred is always there and is the true nature?

2) Shantarakshita questions how all things can be Brahman when beings are in need of liberation. Shankara says we are already Brahman, but our true nature is hidden from us. As someone may mistake a rope for a snake, so we mistake Brahman for the phenomenal world. Shantarakshita similarly believed that since on the absolute level all is the true nature, we are already enlightened. But our true nature is hidden from us as clouds block the sun. We need only remove the obstacles and the true nature will be experienced

Both the Buddhists and Shankara insist that it is our religious practice that will reveal our true nature to us. Having said this, let me reconsider and look more closely at the concepts of momentariness and permanence as they are used by Shantarakshita and Shankara. My hunch is that the real difference between the two philosophers lies not so much in the strict philosophical implications of what they say, as the differing role these two concepts play in their religious practice. Shankara believes that awareness of the ultimate is facilitated by seeing reality as permanent, unchanging. Shantarakshita believes the opposite. The key seems to be the part played by the importance of the elimination of grasping in the Buddhist system. Shantarakshita is convinced that as long as there is anything left to cling to, anything that is seen as permanent, we will not let go of the relative level and achieve the True Nature. Shankara, however, is convinced that seeing everything as the permanent Lord beyond appearances is the best way to enlightenment. What are we to make of this difference

One way of understanding it might be to investigate the role of the sacred person in religious experience. It is no secret that the belief in a personal god generates a tremendous amount of emotional force. Although Shankara stressed contemplation more than bhakti (devotion), he wrote devotional hymns. On the relative level, veneration of Ishvara was of great value in achieving liberation. Is there anything like this in Buddhism?

It was not uncommon in Mahayana Buddhism for the sangha (community) to be encouraged to see all objects as the body of Buddha, all sounds as the words of Buddha, and all thoughts as the thoughts of Buddha. They were sometimes encouraged to see Buddha in every particle and to see all things as composing Buddha. This visualization was a way of breaking down one's ordinary conceptions and replacing them with a mindfulness leading to awareness of the true nature..

Shantarakshita's fellow teacher in Tibet was Guru Padmasambhava. One of the main teachings of this tantric master was Guru Yoga. Not only did this involve profound relationship between teacher and student, but the teacher was seen as the embodiment of Buddha, and the phenomenal world itself as the teacher. This visualization did not depend on the actual phenomenal qualities of the teacher. As long as the teacher was at least moderately wise and compassionate, seeing him or her that way facilitated the process of realization of enlightenment. (Similarly Catholics see the priest at the moment of consecration of the bread and wine as embodying Christ). So the emotional force of veneration of Ishvara in Shankara's system does indeed have a counterpart in Shantarakshita's Guru Yoga. The difference is that Shantarakshita combines the skillful means of Guru Yoga, of seeing reality as the guru with a simultaneous meditation in the momentariness of the ordinary world.

There are, of course, a lot of unanswered questions. How seriously did Shankara mean his "directional use of language" when applied to Brahman?7 Which Buddhists contemporary with him was Shankara actually arguing against? Buddhists kept careful records of their debates with those in their own traditions as well as with those in other traditions. Why have I been unable to find Buddhist debates with Shankara? There is only the legend of the debates he had with Dharmakirti over three lifetimes and ending in the sixth century. 8. How well did he know actual Buddhists? If he knew actual Buddhists,

Shankara and the Problem of Nihilism

might he not have been less hostile? Might he not have realized they were not nihilistic after all? Perhaps someday scholars will be able to answer these questions.

In any case, one biographical note seems to indicate that Shankara, like Shantarakshita, had a similar experience of the compassion of the true nature which transcends all human customs and conventions. For he refused to follow the rules forbidding a sunyasin to perform religious rites for a parent. Out of his compassion he fulfilled his childhood promise to his mother and performed the last rites for her sake.

1. A similar summary of Shankara's critique of Buddhism is to be found in Sengaka Mayeda "Shankara and Buddhism" presented at the International Congress of Vedanta, April 5, 1990, Miami University, Oxford, Ohio.

2. Gaudapada *Gaudapadakarikas* 73-81 P. 161-165, trans. Vidhusekhara, Bhattacharya, University of Calcutta, 1943

3. *Gaudapadakarikas*, op.cit.

4. From *The Conception of Buddhist Nirvana* trans. Th. Stcherbatsky, published by the Academy of Sciences of the U.S.S.R.reprinted in Abelson,R, Friquegnon, M. and Lockwood, M. op.cit. p.108

4

Conclusion

Shantarakshita and the Great Perfection

Summary

Buddha Sakyamuni. initially presented his philosophy as a cure for human suffering. The key to the cure was to be found in the mind. We cannot control all the conditions in the world which produce pain. But we can control our reactions to it. To use a Buddhist analogy, a man does not try to protect his feet by covering a road with leather. Instead he puts leather shoes on his feet.

But how does one control the mind in such a way as to abolish suffering? The answer was the elimination of grasping. One must give up wanting what one does not have and like; and give up wanting to get rid of what one dislikes. Letting go of grasping puts the mind beyond suffering.

It is not so hard to give up the desire for more and more material possessions. Any reasonable person can see that such greediness produces suffering. Renunciation of possessiveness toward loved ones is a much harder form of renunciation. But sooner or later most thoughtful people realize that the inevitability of one's own death and that of the beloved make it irrational to make our happiness dependent on continuous contact with them. Philosophical analysis is merely a tool for making this renunciation easier.

Early Buddhists accepted the reality of the external world. Many believed it to be composed of atoms. But the existence of atoms was a matter of logic, not experience. It seemed clear that since objects are divisible, they must be divisible into "smallest parts". Some Buddhists argued that since we can never have direct knowledge of atoms, they are beyond conception. All we know are sense impressions which result from interacting atoms. As for the subjective realm, the self was considered to be an illusion generated by one's sense impressions. Internal sensations thoughts, images etc., succeed each other with such rapidity and similarity that they generate the illusion of "same self". But there are no substantial selves. Nor are there substantial objects. Rather there is a temporal river of ever changing atoms, sense impressions, feelings thoughts etc.

Although changing, the external world was still thought of as real. Later Buddhist philosophers such as Nagarjuna believed it would be useful to show the unreality of atoms etc. because if one does not believe in the reality of a thing, one might be less likely to view it as desirable.

And so the Madhyamika school of Buddhism was born. A series of arguments resembling Zeno's paradoxes, were produced to show the contradictions in the concept of an atom. For example, if an atom is the smallest possible thing it must be indivisible. But to be indivisible the extension of an atom must be zero. Any higher value is divisible. But if the extension is zero, then atoms cannot be the building blocks of the universe, for zero plus zero is always zero. Even the reality of causal relations was called into question. If cause and effect are identical, then everything should happen at once; -events cannot be successive, because this would necessitate a separate cause for each effect to bring it about at one specific time rather than another. And cause and effect cannot be different because if the cause precedes the effect it must occupy a different moment in time. So if only the present moment exists, when the cause is present the effect is in a yet non-existent future, and when the effect is present, the cause is in an already non-existent past. The cause must act on the effect to bring it about but cannot because they are in separate temporal moments.

The Mahdyamika school was followed by the Chittamatra (or "consciousness only" school) the principle philosophers of which . were Asanga and Vasibandhu. These philosophers, while continuing the Buddhist tradition that there is no substantial self, nonetheless argued that the fact of mental experience is inescapable. The mind knows what is given to it in sensation. The mind knows the principles of logic. But if all is mind, how can there be a distinction between subject and object? Their favorite explanation was through an analogy with a dream. In a dream one's mind produces surprising novel experiences. Yet who would deny that the dream object is mental. Why are our experiences alike (person to person) if they are mental? Because they are produced by similar mental habits. The system of mental inter-dependent co-origination was called the alaya.

Shantarakshita unified the Madhyamika and Chittamatra (also known as Yogachara) points of view. He repeated and extended the ancient arguments against the reality of matter. So it would seem that if reality is not material, it must be mental. Shantarakshita, however, shows that the attempt to link up mental states with mental objects on a one to one basis is hopelessly confused. And so is the attempt to make mind, which is subjectivity, into an object of thought at all. So ultimately mind itself must be understood as being beyond conception.

Shantarakshita speaks of the Madhyamika and Chittamatra schools as the two chariots, holding the reins of which leads to enlightenment. The correct way to understand the philosophical situation is in terms of both. One must begin with the mental, the impure relativistic knowledge of the world. This is based on distinctions, one term of which cannot be meaningful without its opposite. There is no cold without hot,- - no subject without object, -- no cause without effect- - no existence without non-existence. The meaning of these terms is relative to a specific context. (To put it in Berkeleyan terms, what is fast to a tortoise is not fast to a hare.) On this level, Shantarakshita could well be termed a pragmatic realist.

Then one must consider that all these distinctions are made relative to a human way of dividing up the world into categories. We think in terms of space and time and we divide up our world into minutes and objects. Thus we have number. We grasp at things; -thus we create the illusion of enduring persons who can continue to possess objects. Realizing this, we see all things as an activity of mind. This is the pure relative truth.

Finally, we realize we know mind inauthentically, that is as object, rather than subject. But if mind is really awareness and can never be an object, we can never know it in terms of categories. The nature of mind is itself beyond conception. It is emptiness. That is the absolute truth.

It is important to realize that the absolute and the relative are not two separate realms. The relative is just the absolute seen from the relative point of view. This is what is meant in the Heart Sutra when it is said that "Form is emptiness, emptiness is form". The further the mind progresses in giving up distinctions, categories etc. the closer it comes to absolute awareness. So the relative is not the enemy of the absolute, but the way in which it can be realized. This is the point of the *Tattvasiddhi,*

Shantarakshita and Dzogchen

To return to the early Buddhist conception of Nirvana ,while indeed the elimination of craving does produce the absence of suffering, and even a kind of peace, why should the bodhisattvas speak of it as being so blissfully wonderful? Why doesn't the extinction of desire lead to a kind of stoic calm rather than such perfect joyful fulfillment? The answer to this question provides the raison d'etre of Dzogchen.

According to Dzogchen there is something about the true nature that lends itself to being experienced in a way that is productive of perfect bliss,-- a bliss that overflows into wise and compassionate activity. This is not something that is provably true. It is a perspective,- an experience of a special kind. But although it is special in terms of ordinary sentient beings, it is the normal, natural way of experiencing reality.

We are prevented from having this experience because of the grasping nature of ordinary mind. Failing to understand the inherent emptiness of all things, we grasp at them. Failing to get what we want, we become angry, jealous, fearful, full of hate. Our perception is distorted and impoverished. Through the practice of selflessness, loving kindness, compassion and meditation, these poisons are overcome. As the mind relaxes it is prepared to learn to see in a new way.

Since mind is simply the relative side of the true nature, it can be transformed in such a way as to be a pure reflection of the absolute. To do this, special skills are necessary. These are the inner tantric practices: maha, anu and ati yoga.

The outer tantras involve external practices such as breathing, fasting or control of diet etc. The inner practices are forms of mental training. They are complex, but briefly they may be described as follows: a) Maha yoga is the visualization of the world as the palace of a deity. A glass of water becomes nectar. A chair becomes a throne. maha yoga is designed to sensitize the mind to the special qualities of the pure relative truth. Anu yoga is similar to maha yoga, except that it focuses on the visualization of one's body as the body of the deity. Certain channels, winds, drops of nectar are visualized in the process of purification.

Finally in the highest yoga, ati yoga, the heart of Dzogchen, everything is left as it is. Nothing is seen as other than as it is perceived, yet this "ordinary world" is experienced in a special way that cannot be described in words.

Now to return to the *Tattvasiddhi*. Although this work does not mention the three inner tantras by name, their use is implied in this work. On the pure relative level, it is possible to make use of certain causal conditions which produce special results leading to enlightenment. Having already purified the mind of the poisons of ignorance and fear, anger and hatred, jealousy and attachment, and, through the practice of philosophy realized the emptiness of all forms, the practitioner is ready to use the manure of the city in the farmyards of the countryside. The practice of the six paramitas, generosity, effort, patience, morality, mindfulness and wisdom have ensured that this "manure" will not be misused.

What is this "manure"? It is the worldly practices involving desire which were considered necessary to renounce in traditional monastic Buddhism. Chief among these is sexual union. In the *Tattvasiddhi*, referred to as "touch," it becomes an experience leading to enlightenment.

Shantarakshita, of course, is not referring to sexual union as it is practiced by ordinary people. It has to be transformed by the mind. It becomes, through this transformation, a living symbol of the unity of . form and emptiness, of wisdom and compassion.

Why is this "great seal" so essential in the production of awareness of the true nature, of enlightenment itself? Shantarakshita argues that on the relative level, like causes produce like effects. The result of enlightenment is a state of ecstatic bliss. One can never prepare the way for this through painful ascetic practices. They will only sadden and confuse the mind. The joy of union, however, is in some ways similar to awareness of the true nature. In this joy, all distinctions seem to disappear. Lover and beloved seem to flow into each other. Subject and object as distinct entities seem to melt away.

Fear and grasping cause clinging to the beloved and more and more sorrow. But in the great seal, the partners visualize each other as god and goddess, form and emptiness, wisdom and compassion. The experience of union becomes a meditation on the true nature. So the great seal becomes a special cause productive of of enlightenment. The absence of craving precludes the onset of suffering. The great seal establishes the yogi and yogini more and more firmly in the awareness of the true nature. But this practice is one that goes beyond sensation to reveal the bliss of wisdom rather than emotion.

In the *Tathvasiddhi,* Shantarakshita offers a transcendental argument for the possibility of the attainment of enlightenment. But of course, it cannot be proved that anyone has actually achieved enlightenment in this way. This is a "try and see" procedure for those who have already achieved a high degree of realization through the elimination of poisons and the practice of virtue.

Why can it not be proved that anyone has ever reached enlightenment? This brings us back to the nature of Dzogchen. And I believe Wittgensteinian perspectivism has provided us with a conceptual framework for understanding Dzogchen.

In the *Philosophical Investigations,* Wittgenstein illustrates his ideas about perspectives through the duck/rabbit example.. Given a certain illustration, one can see it as either a duck or a rabbit. Sometimes people can only see the duck or only the rabbit. If they can only see one, we might call them "aspect blind".

In his book *Philosophy of Art*[1], Virgil Aldrich uses this example of the duck/rabbit to illustrate problems about what one sees when one sees a picture. There is, for Aldrich, a root sense of a thing. But we never know things in this root sense. Things always appear to us under one aspect or another.

Take a painting, for example. If the painting is large, men moving it may very likely ignore its beauty and concentrate on its physical aspects; its weight and shape. The critic watching them move it may be oblivious to its physical aspects but enchanted by its grace and proportion, its aesthetic aspects. Someone who could not see the painting from this aesthetic perspective, we might consider "aspect blind". Since perception of beauty is a normal human ability, we might ask why this person's perception is blocked. Perhaps if the viewer hates religion, and the painting has a religious subject, this hatred may make the viewer incapable of appreciating the painting's grace and dynamlsm. Removal of this hatred might free the "aesthetic eye" of a beholder.

Virgil Aldrich's application of Wittgensteinian perspectivism to art could be extended, to psychology and morality as well. Autistic children, because of fear or other causes, may be unable to see other people as people. They are incapable of taking the psychological perspective, Great kindness and patience in working with these children may occasionally result in a lifting of the barriers to the normal psychologicl point of view. Holding the hand of another child, putting on the clothes of another, may all be learning devices which prepare the way for the interpersonal psychological experience.

Moral awareness may also be blocked in some people. The ethical point of view, considered so normal, may not be part of the experience of criminals described by the police as moral idiots. Such people do not knowingly choose to perform wrong actions rather than right. They see the world in terms of practical expediency and not in terms of morality at all. They fail to see the moral picture.

So far I have described a series of perspectives - physical object, aesthetic, psychological and moral. Perspectives are neither true nor false. At most they can be considered apt or inapt. It is true that certain things lend themselves to be perceived in certain ways more easily than others. Monet's water lily paintings are easier to see as aesthetic objects than a toaster. But we couldn't prove that someone who saw a toaster as beautiful was wrong. As Descartes pointed out, we cannot prove the being we see walking outside the window wearing a coat and hat is a person like ourselves and not an automaton. Yet it seems apt to say this is indeed a perspective.

The Dzogchen masters are claiming that there is an additional perspective we can take on being and that this perspective is indeed more apt than any other. They cannot describe this perspective to those who do not share it, any more than we could describe the aesthetic perspective (or moral perspective) to someone incapable of taking these points of view. Similarly, to those of us incapable of taking the enlightened perspective, such a perspective seems beyond our ken.

The analysis, however, cannot be pushed too far. Buddhists claim that enlightenment is in principle beyond conception, because all conceptions involve distinctions. And the state of enlightenment is beyond distinction. On the aesthetic level one can distinguish between paintings that are static and those which are dynamic. But one could not distinguish enlightenment qualities, except in terms of the varying effects of the meditation on the meditator.

Thus Dzogchen masters insist that the enlightenment state is not nothingness, but is filled with qualities. Here the rational mind must leave off because we cannot imagine a fullness of being that is beyond distinctions. Perhaps when we reach such a level we will understand.

What reason do we have to suppose such a level is reachable,- - that there is such a level at all? To have reason to believe in the existence of enlightenment, there must be points of access to it long before it has been actually reached. This is called by some Buddhist writers the tathatagarbha, or seed of enlightenment. There are examples of the bliss of enlightenment in ordinary experience, such as the objectless joy of the happy child,- - and in adult life, those precious moments of tranquillity when one feels at one with the universe,-- or even as Karl Jaspers suggests, when one has gone through a tragic experience and been strengthened by it. Such intimations serve as assurance that the search for enlightenment is not the pursuit of an imaginary goal, and why the achievment of this goal should lead to bliss rather than indifference. Further evidence is provided by the aura of radiant happiness and compassion of the great teachers.

The most the philosopher can do is suggest that Dzogchen constitutes a philosophically coherent view of religious experience, one in which a perspectival shift has been substituted for faith in doctrines. Whether or not that shift is possible, or whether reality is objectively of such a nature as to be experienced this way must be decided for themselves by those who set out on this path.

Shantarakshita's Significance

I began this study with the claim that Shantarakshita stands at the culminating point of a tradition, in a way similar to Immanuael Kant. There is indeed a striking similarity between the two philosophers. Both divide knowledge into the absolute (noumenal) and relative (phenomenal) levels, considering the absolute as a regulative principle rather than an object of knowledge. Both rejected skepticism, sense data theory and idealism.

There is even a similarity in their vision of the noumenal in a religious way. In the last analysis in *The Critique of Pure Reason,* Kant refuses to distinguish between substance, the transcendental self and God. Kant sees God as the ultimate unifying principle, itself unknowable, which unifies substance and soul:

> ...if I think of a being as existing which corresponds to a mere idea, and a transcendental one, I ought not to admit the existence of such a being by itself, because no concepts through which I can conceive any object definitely, can reach it, and the conditions of the objective validity of my concepts are excluded by the idea itself. The concepts of reality, of substance, even of

Conclusion

causality, and those of necessity in existence, have no meaning that could determine any object, unless they are used to make the empirical knowledge of an object possible. They may be used, therefore, to explain the possibility of things in the world of sense, but not to explain the possibility of a *universe itself,* because such an hypothesis is outside the world and could never be an object of possible experience. I can, however, admit perfectly well such an inconceivable Being, being an object of a mere idea, relative to the world of sense, though not as existing by itself."[2]

For Shantarakshita, the attainment of emptiness is the goal of religion (dharma). Unlike Kant, however, he sees the tantra as the "skillful means" needed to immerse oneself in non-conceptual awareness. Kant would have rejected the possibility of any awareness of the noumenal, because for him concepts were inescapable.

Shantarakshita's understanding of language, as we have seen, is rather close to that of Wittgenstein, for, on the relative level, he identifies non-vacuous contrast as the touchstone of meaning. And as Kant responded critically to Berkeley, Shantarakshita rejects, on the ultimate level the vision of world as idea. His view that Nirvana and Samsara are two different perspectives is suggestive of Spinoza.

His criticism of a necessary connection between cause and effect and his affirmation of the bundle theory of the self are similar to that of David Hume. His theory of language will be echoed later in the work of Wittgenstein. He is truly a philosopher for all seasons.

1. Aldrich, Virgil *Philosophy of Art* Englewood Cliffs:Prentice Hall,1963

2. Kant, Immanuel *Critique of Pure Reason* (The Elements of Transcendentalism, Appendix) trans. Max Muller New York: Dolphin Macmillan,1961 pp. 399-400

BIBLIOGRAPHY

Aldrich, Virgil *Philosophy of Art* Englewood Cliffs: Prentice Hall, 1963

Anacker, Stefan *Seven Works of Vasubandhu : The Buddhist Psychological Doctor* Delhi: Motilal Banarsidass, 1998

Bhattacharya, B. Foreward to the *Tattasamgraha* in *Tattvasamgraha of Santaraksita* Baroda: Oriental Institute, 1984

Isayeva, Natalia *Shankara and Indian Philosophy* Albany: SUNY Press, 1993

Kant, Immanuel *The Critique of Pure Reason* trans. Muller, F.Max Garden City: Dolphin Macmillan, 1961

Kapstein, Matthew "The Fallacies of Personalistic Vitalism" *Journal of Indian Philosophy* Dordrecht Holland: D. Reidel Vol 17 March, 1989 pp. 43-59

Lopez Jr., Donald *Svatantrika* Ithaca: Snow Lion, 1987

Nagarjuna *The Fundamental Wisdom of the Middle Way* translation and commentary by Garfield, Jay L. Oxford: Oxford University Press, 1995

Ramanuja, *The Vedanta Sutra* trans. Thibault, George. Delhi: Motilal Banarsidass, 1966

Santaraksita *Madhyamakalankara* and *Tattvasiddhi* translation and commentary by Ven Khenchen Palden Sherab Rinpoche and Ven Khenpo Tsewang Dongyal Rinpoche forthcoming Boca Raton: Skydancer Press

Tattvasamgraha vols. 1&2 trans. Jha, Ganganatha Delhi: Motilal Banarsidass, 1937

Sarachcandra, Edirivira R. "From Vasubandhu to Santaraksita" *Journal of Indian Philosophy* vol.4 no. 1/2 Sept./ Dec., 1976 pp.70-107

Sherab (Rinpoche), Ven. Khenchen Palden *Ceaseless Echoes of Great Silence: A Commentary on the Heart Sutra* trans. Dongyal (Rinpoche),Ven. Khenpo Tsewang Boca Raton: Sky Dancer, 1993

Smart, Ninian *Doctrine and Argument in Indian Philosophy* London, 1964

Snellgrove, David *Indo-Tibetan Buddhism* vols 1&2 Boston: Shambhala, 1987

Wittgenstein, Ludwig *Philosophical Investigations* trans. Anscombe, G. New York: Macmillan, 1953